In 1921, Aleksandr Rodchenko exhibited his monochrome canvases of red, yellow, and blue, apparently intending to reference nothing, to kill painting's formal value simply by cutting the lifeline to its own history. This, he later said, would lead to its logical conclusion: "Every plane is a plane and there is to be no representation."[1] Distilling "form" from history in Palestine often feels just as impossible a task as Rodchenko's, because history has a way of growing its roots through no matter how hard one tries to momentarily suspend it.

I once told the activist and Jaffa expert Sami Abu Shehadeh that I only knew Tel Aviv from the pages of coffee-table books on architecture. "Then you don't know Jaffa," he replied, "if you have not walked Tel Aviv." "But I walk Jaffa," I insisted. In retrospect, my interest in tracing modern architecture in Palestine might have been to find resolve: How are the significations of postwar modernist gems—that my partner Tirdad Zolghadr radically opened my eyes to in Berlin ten years ago—subverted in a heartbeat in the Palestinian context? Not unlike the unnamed actress in Marguerite Duras's *Hiroshima mon amour* (1959), I simply cannot "see" those very same lines within Israel; in part because building the State of Israel was aggressively intertwined with transforming Palestine into a Jewish nation-state through the strategic erasure of an architectural time and place, in order to make way for a Zionist one.[2]

Between 2013 and 2015, I spontaneously recorded any instances of cubical, circular, flat, straight, blunt, or unornamented architectural forms in the Palestinian urban landscape whenever I saw them. The images I took along the way were unashamedly skewed by their planes and perspectives. They celebrate a subjective gaze, and more importantly, prioritize mobility and movement as a device against Israeli checkpoints and blockades designed to disenfranchise and isolate Palestinian communities from each other.

Halfway through this project, in the spring of 2014, I taught a documentary theory course that took the very building that housed us as a point of departure: Al-Quds University's Institute of Modern Media, a wonderful modernist structure that was once the Hilton Carlton of Ramallah. Since then, a more social, subjective, and historical reading began to evolve, which was most influenced by the curator, writer, and architect Yazid Anani. Through various collaborations between the different universities we teach in, he has shown me how buildings tell stories.

By 2015, I was invited by the Riwaq Biennale to reflect on the institutional history of Riwaq through a two-year durational project using my images as material for a book. Riwaq is an organization working with communities to document, preserve, and restore Palestinian architectural heritage under occupation. Their work was celebrated in 2006 with the publication of a wonderfully thick and rich register of historic, potentially endangered buildings in the West Bank, East Jerusalem, and Gaza; but this register ends in 1948.

I understood from Riwaq that an incredible trio—Sahar Qawasmi, Mouhanad Hadid, and Iyad Issa—had worked hard ten years ago, to compile a new Riwaq compendium of modernist architectural types, but the project was yet to be completed due to life meanderings to other cities and places. I therefore wish to thank the director of Riwaq, Khaldun Bshara, for his infectious optimism and belief that an artist's book can be a step toward a registry of the modernist cultural heritage of occupied Palestine, and for his approach toward the adaptive reuse of such spaces rather than their potential demolition. I also wish to thank Rima Alkeilani, for her charming stride in helping me navigate various sites in Nablus, and also Zahraa Zawawi, who complicated my notions of "heritage" when she walked me through Falasteen Street, around Cinema Al-Assi in downtown Nablus, where the Latin convent and its communities once stood. In 1952 the mayor of Nablus, Naim Abdel Hadi, had demolished the entire area to make way for a new urban sprawl, which is now a breathtaking series of midcentury facades.

Many thanks to the Ghosheh family as well as the Kanaan, Qutob, and Aloul families for their generosity and their knowledge of the architectural histories of their homes. Similarly, I wish to thank Naseer Arafat, Charles Issa Kidess, and Ayman Shakaa as well as George Arbid, Sahar Qawasmi, Fida Touma, Felicity Scott, Katia Sanders, and Philip Hopper, for their commentary. Thanks also to Laura Napier for her color corrections on a small excerpt of this project, which was shown in a poignant exhibition at the Centre for Contemporary Arts, Glasgow, titled “The Shame of Victory,” curated by Remco de Blaaij—who was instrumental in the beginning of this project. And thanks to Tanya Habjouqa and Yazan Khalili for solving a few problems I had along the way. Finally, I am grateful for the support of the University of Oxford's Ruskin School of Art, the research support of St John's College in particular, and, most importantly, for the financial support of Mophradat, without which this book would not have been possible.

What surfaced from this process and what, specifically, is shown in this publication is a compilation of printed matter in and around architecture, from the late 1940s to the early 1970s, produced in the occupied and highly strangulated cities of Nablus, Jerusalem, Bethlehem, Ramallah, and Jericho. The time frame is bounded by the creation of Israel in 1948 and the war of 1967, when the rest of Palestine was annexed to Israel. During that time, this terrain, otherwise known as the West Bank, came under Jordanian rule. A host of interesting buildings built before 1948 in Jaffa and Haifa (even Lydda and Ramle) have therefore been left out; Elias al-Murr's 1937 Cinema al-Hamra in Jaffa, now the Scientology Center of Tel Aviv, is perhaps the best known. Furthermore, the city of Gaza and the homes of expelled Palestinians now residing in refugee camps on the West Bank under the mandate of UNRWA were also left out. (Even though these homes were eventually instituted, memorized—even memorialized—in pure concrete in refugee camps, where the enduring colonial British law that still requires 80 percent of facades to be built from "native stone" does *not* stand.)[3]

This book is intentionally anti-chronological, anti-typological, and anti-indexical. From the start, I did not seek to prove the existence of an architectural modernist "movement" as such—in part because if there ever was one (*anywhere*, for that matter), the Palestinian case was clearly stunted and amputated: first by the larger Zionist settler-colonial project that itself appropriated Bauhaus architecture, and more recently by Palestinian neoliberalism in the guise of an independence movement. There was, indeed, a strong appeal to modern forms freshly learned in Cairo, variations of which were being implemented in Baghdad, Beirut, and later Khartoum via economical means and local technologies.[4] But the ethos did not seem to have been rationally, socially, or ideologically driven. Rather, it was an organic growth out of vernacular building codes and post-Ottoman styles that had already begun to use simplified forms (for example, concrete slab and steel systems allowing for flat roofs).[5] Also significant here is the influence of the International Style as *style* spreading through print media out of Cairo,[6] in addition to the growing discourse on national (and native) cultural identity, materiality, and the adequacy of limestone and its abundance in Palestine's mountainous terrain. Finally, the potential and currency of negotiating around laws and bylaws requiring the use of local stone on buildings' facades. Architects navigated restrictions on concrete facades on an individual basis, under an occupation regime that heavily restricted the issuing of building permits,[7] by advocating for a green space here, or the first commercial elevator in town there—as in the case of Barghouti Architects' Hananiah & Kharaz Building in Ramallah.[8] Figures I have not mentioned and who deserve separate treatment include Diran Voskeritchian, Anis Srouji, Mohammad

Hijazi, Mammon Nahas, and, more recently, the incredible Senan Abdelqader, whose theories and designs in Jerusalem and Israel are continuously evolving in spite of explicit depopulation strategies targeting Palestinian communities.[9]

I am most grateful to the architect Reema Arafat for guiding me through her late father Hani 's work, and for showing me just how many of the buildings that I was interested in were his designs. I am also grateful to the architects Rizek Khoury in Ramallah and Fouad Sayegh in Amman for inspiring me and speaking to me about their life's work; and, always, to the late Jafar Tukan, who once told me that peeping through the roof lanterns of hammams in Nablus as a kid and giggling with his friends was when he first "got" architecture. Here I also wish to reference my colleague Dani Leventhal's musings on subjectivity; Tom Nicholson's sentimental and tender book *Comparative Monument (Ma'man Allah)* (2014), on the Mamilla Cemetery in West Jerusalem; and Natascha Sadr Haghighian, for her organic approach to artist's books at large.

Further still, I am indebted to Khaled Hourani, Nicola Perugini, Hoda Rouhana, Inass Yassin, Casey Asprooth-Jackson, Shorooq Harb, Mohanad Yaqubi, Emilio Dabed, Vera Tamari, Yazid Anani, Sandi Hilal, Sharif Waked, Hassan Jabareen, Fadi Abu Nemeh, and Alessandro Petti for the marks each has left on my thinking in the past few years, and thus on this book. Many thanks to Ala Younis for holding my hand and finally showing me the finish line. And, last but not least, to the sociologist Salim Tamari, whose mutually loving and relentless approach to archival materials and social histories has changed me, and to whom I chose to address this book.

Finally, I have drawn most energy from watching my little one, Soraya, toddle every morning on the Art Deco tiles of the 1933 Ajlouny House in Ramallah Tahta. A colossal home with curved balconies in pink Bethlehem stone overlooking fruit orchards (without a single water hose on the land). And so for their support, always, I thank my family: Tirdad, Alia, Hanan, Randa, Ala Toukan, Haya Ghanma, Abed Azzam, and Violet Ajlouny, my landlord, who became family.

1 "The Death of Painting," exhibition text for the retrospective "Aleksandr Rodchenko," Museum of Modern Art, New York, 1998, https://www.moma.org/interactives/exhibitions/1998/rodchenko/texts/death_of_painting.html. See also *Alexander Rodchenko: 1891–1956*, exh. cat., ed. David Elliott (Oxford: Museum of Modern Art, 1979).

2 Refer to Sharon Rotbard's seminal book *White City, Black City: Architecture and War in Tel Aviv and Jaffa* (Cambridge, MA: MIT Press, 2015) on the myths of Tel Aviv's Bauhaus architecture, which was instrumentalized in the erasure of Jaffa. See also Eyal Sivan's 2009 documentary *Jaffa, the Orange's Clockwork* and Decolonizing Architecture's research

on Tel Aviv's Etzel Museum, which was built on the ruins of Jaffa's obliterated al-Manshiyya neighborhood (Alessandro Petti, Sandi Hilal, and Eyal Weizman, *Architecture after Revolution* [Berlin: Sternberg Press, 2013]).

3 See Nasser Abourahme, "Assembling and Spilling-Over: Towards an 'Ethnography of Cement' in a Palestinian Refugee Camp," *International Journal of Urban and Regional Research* 39, no. 2 (March 2015), 200–17.

4 George Arbid, interviewed by Deen Sharp, "The Arab Center for Architecture (ACA): Interview with George Arbid," *Jadaliyya*, September 29, 2015, http://www.jadaliyya.com/pages/index/22764/the-arab-center-for-architecture-(aca)_interview-wn.

5 See Shadia Yousef Touqan, "Urban Development under Prolonged Military Occupation: The Case of Nablus/Palestine" (PhD diss., Bartlett School of Architecture, University College London, 1995); and Naseer R. Arafat, *Nablus: City of Civilizations* (Nablus: Cultural Heritage Enrichment Center, 2012).

6 Indeed, one of the conclusions of Bernard Khoury and George Arbid's project at the Venice Biennale's 14th International Architecture Exhibition was that "while some of the featured [buildings] can be perceived as inspiring applications of the modernist principles, others can be considered symptomatic of the tendency to embrace modernism as a trend rather than a project." Bernard Khoury, "Fundamentalists and Other Arab Modernisms," Divisare website, January 18, 2016, https://divisare.com/projects/307953-bernard-khoury-delfino-sisto-legnani-fundamentalists-and-other-arab-modernisms. See also the exhibition catalogue, *Architecture from the Arab World: 1914–2014 (A Selection),* ed. George Arbid (Manama: Ministry of

Culture of Bahrain; Beirut: Arab Center for Architecture, 2014). On the influence of print media on architecture at the time, see Mohamed Elshahed's fascinating excavations of architectural publications in Egypt from 1936 to 1967: Mohamed Elshahed, "Revolutionary Modernism? Architecture and the Politics of Transition in Egypt 1936–1967" (PhD diss., New York University, 2015), ProQuest 3685862.

7 Mouhanad Hadid, "Architectural Styles Survey in Palestinian Territories" (August 2002), Ministry of Local Government, Palestine National Authority, http://www.molg.pna.ps/ecb/studies/architecture/arch.pdf.

8 I am grateful to Khaldun Bshara for sharing this and other anecdotes about the building, which is included here, in the series "Blue Sky Thinking," even though it falls slightly outside the time frame of my selection.

9 See Senan Abdelqader, *Architecture of (in)Dependency*, Israeli Presentation Catalogue, 7th International Architecture Biennial in São Paulo, 2007, http://www.senanarchitects.com/architecture-of-dependency.

Pages 18 and 19:
A photographer's view of the radio towers during the opening of the International Broadcasting Station in Ramallah, 1939

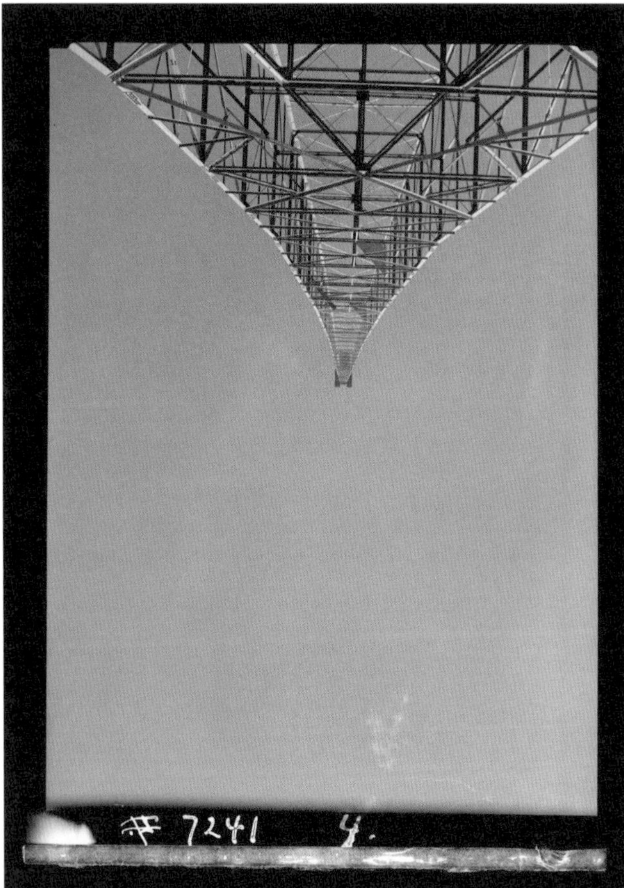
7241 4.

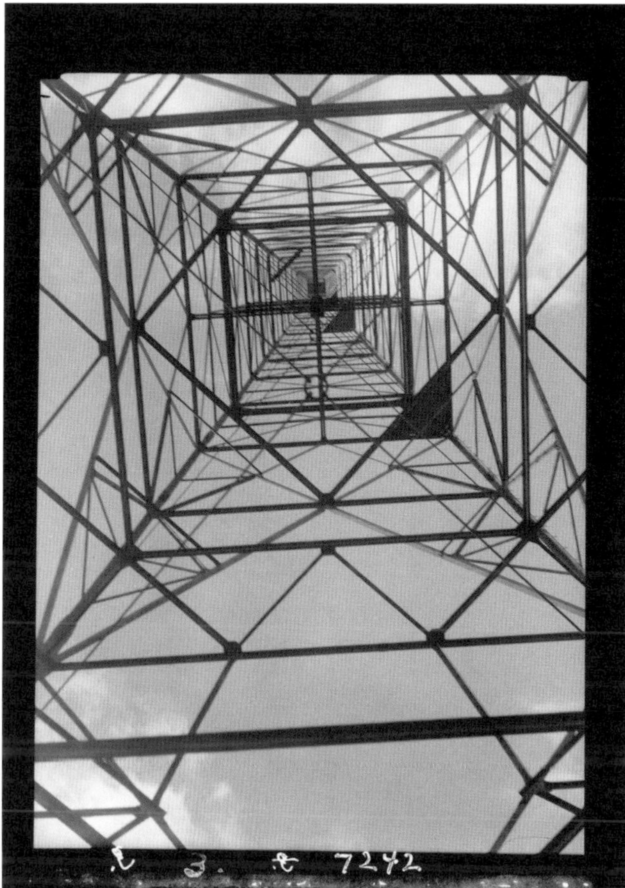
7242

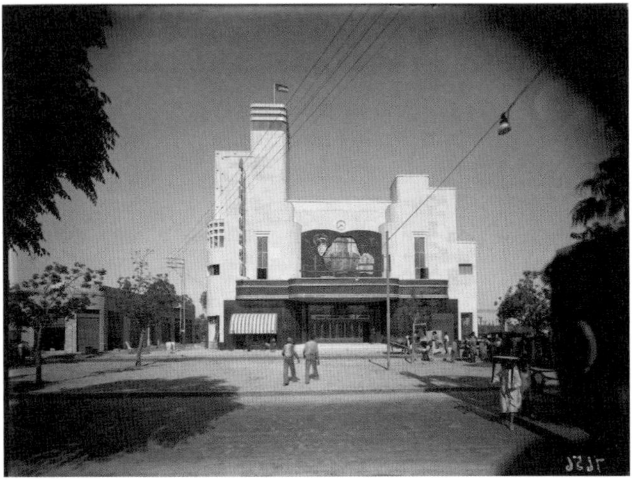

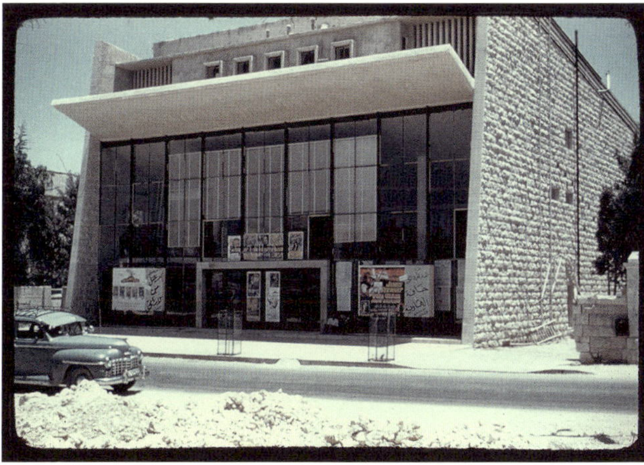

Pages 20 and 21:
Cinema al-Hamra, Jaffa,
Jamal Basha Street, 1937 (left)
Cinema al-Hamra, Jerusalem,
Salah ad-Din Street 1953 (right)

Dear Salim,

Here is the image I was looking for in my phone when I told you that I often recall your lecture in Ramallah in July 2015 on Jerusalem as a "pickled city." You drew this amazing picture in my mind of British colonial administrators (McLean, Ashbee, and Storrs) walking through Jerusalem complaining of a "stench" while trying to measure its corners—ironically, in order to preserve it—like any other museum acquisition.[10] *I think of these characters every day here in Oxford; two by two, with tape measures and clipboards in their arms, they roam the college quads and fill out forms. Men in black, always in pairs.*

While presenting a version of my work Material for a Book on Palestinian Modernism *in Glasgow, I found out that Sir William McLean was also a member of the Scottish Unionist Party. As you explain in your essay "City of Riffraff," McLean was the city engineer for the British Colonial Office.*[11] *In 1918, he was called in for a visit from his post in Alexandria to come up with a comprehensive master plan for the city of Jerusalem. In a matter of two months, McLean miraculously proposed a set of policies that continue to govern the building code of a significant part of the urban fabric of what is now "occupied Palestine," or what Suad Amiry terms "Minor Palestine" (the West Bank, East Jerusalem, and the Gaza Strip).*[12] *The most enduring of these laws and bylaws requires that facades in the West Bank and Jerusalem be made of "native stone," even when stone is no longer a structural element but a decorative one: a cover for hollow concrete blocks and steel; usually ultrathin, deep-quarried, machine-cut, and white-polished.*[13]

At that same symposium, another lecturer, Yazeed El Rifai, practically skipped over the entire period from 1948 to Fayyadism in 2007, when bank loans were allowed under Prime Minister Salam Fayyad, prompting the current real estate frenzy in Ramallah. He seamlessly mapped out wonderful anecdotes of the first wave of Palestinian emigration to the Americas out of Ramallah in the nineteenth century, and the wave of US missionaries in. He rushed over the era I am interested in with a powerpoint slide titled "The 50's & 60's [sic]." I often think of this extra s (or in this case, apostrophe s), that we add to connote plurality of years. Why does it feel like a record between two wars under Jordanian rule that stutters every time we wish to hear it? Why do you think this period is so inaudible?

I would love to know what it means to you as a social historian—who, in my mind, thrives in the vaults of uncommon archives, researching incredible, eyebrow-raising figures in the modern Palestinian city—that

I keep taking pictures without any people in them. Many of these buildings have been visibly depopulated by war and flux. In some instances, though, I consciously depopulate the people that stay in my frame. I have this urge to discard an image with a person in it or tilt up my viewfinder so that I don't see them. The least interesting proposition in Roland Barthes's vast body of work was his thesis on the studium *of a photograph, the element that pierces us "like an arrow" and helps us to situate and read it: "The photographer teaches me how the Russians dress."*[14] *The person behind the lens suddenly becomes an informer, who should provide an "education" of some sort to the viewer flipping through pages to imagine a place: "I note a boy's big cloth cap, another's necktie."*[15] *The Palestinian refugee, in particular, eventually became the pluperfect camera subject of a place imagined through images of itself. What would happen if we depopulate the picture, the sign? And not the thing itself, the place, but merely its referent—the photograph of it, which was itself fled, evicted, and replaced in parts.*

Bertolt Brecht famously argued that a photograph of a factory tells us little about what is happening inside that factory.[16] *Neither does it tell of the class or labor relations that impose the very order we see in its representation. The fact of the matter is that I too came out with singular, flat, frontal, depopulated renditions of architectural exteriors, especially of the quintessential bourgeois icon: the villa. If I were to caption many of them, they would read: "Villa Kanaan," "Villa Aloul," "Villa Qutob," "Villa Salti," "Villa Mikhail," etc. What is the context that could explain this architectural obsession with the villa? When did consumer culture first begin to idealize the single-family dwelling as a way of escaping Jerusalem or Nablus's old city?*

Obviously, I have not forgotten the backdrop of war and colonial struggle, and that municipal architects like Hani Arafat ended up with gaps in their CVs from time in prison or being refused reentry after travels abroad. Nor have I forgotten that independence projects all over the world brought with them funding for architects to experiment with stadiums, public housing, museums, hospitals, and libraries, let alone the European architects finally facing the future after World War II. But when experimentation did happen in our context, it seemed to be mostly hotels or private, fully detached single-family homes, and just in this period of "respite" (only to be, oddly, immediately replicated in Amman after the 1967 war).

Photography has always been the double-edged object and subject of architecture. Owen Hatherley writes that the modernist building began to respond to the photographic record of itself by becoming more photogenic, that the advent of color film influenced the addition of color and monochromatic tones to buildings' facades.[17] *Meanwhile, David Campany builds on Walter Benjamin's assertion "that the kind of art [and architecture] that will triumph will be that which looks good in photographic reproduction," proposing that the cultural value of architecture is invented by its camera image.*[18]

Exterior value aside, it seems we have also chosen to alter the interior worlds of these buildings and the stories they once told. Three years ago, I stayed up until midnight with the Ghosheh family, looking through their photographs of the Hilton Carlton hotel that their late father, Dr. Mohammad Ghosheh, opened between Ramallah and Jerusalem. I remember seeing pictures of dancers on tour from Casino-du-Liban on the first-ever piste in town, where Petula Clark might have also performed "Colour My

World."[19] I saw men in intense discussions at the bar and women in beautiful party dresses. I gathered the pictures into a pile to bring back to class to show my students, who were making works about this building. One of the brothers insisted that I come back the next day, so that they would have time to count the photographs and get them in order. I returned the next morning and found that my pile had turned in to photographs of religious figures in official conferences in the banquet hall, waiters serving tables, and happy families. Maybe this erasure was critical. Maybe they understood that students would post just another photograph on social media that joyfully screams, "Look → we were once modern!"

So where does "modernity" begin for you in your work? Does it really have an hour, like dawn over darkness? Always late, "be-late"?[20] There is a wonderful allegory in my mind of Robert J. Flaherty's 1922 silent film, Nanook of the North. *Flaherty wanted to document the life of an Inuit family. The problem was his camera wouldn't fit inside their igloo. A larger structure was built for him, but the dome kept collapsing. When he finally succeeded, the interior of the igloo was too dark to film. In the end, the subjects of the film, Nanook and his family, built and lived in a three-sided, open igloo just for the camera—to help us imagine their interior spaces. My own process of narrating a story of Palestinian modernism has been quite similar: the story collapses the moment I attempt to seamlessly represent it.*

I'm looking forward to seeing you,

Oraib

10 C. R. Ashbee, Jerusalem's "civic advisor" after World War I, wrote, "The impulse of the Moslem when he built was always different from ours. He never thought things out either in structure or in policy. He picked up the beautiful fragments, botched them together, made an exquisite pattern work that should help dreaming, then sat down and dreamed." Quoted in Nicholas E. Roberts, "Dividing Jerusalem: British Urban Planning in the Holy City," *Journal of Palestine Studies* 42, no. 4 (Summer 2013), 14.

11 Salim Tamari, "City of Riffraff: Crowds, Public Space, and New Urban Sensibilities in War-Time Jerusalem, 1917–1921," in *Comparing Cities: The Middle East and South Asia*, ed. Kamran Asdar Ali and Martina Rieker (Oxford: Oxford University Press, 2010).

12 Suad Amiry, "Interview with Suad Amiry," in *The Arab City: Architecture and Representation*, ed. Amale Andraos and Nora Akawi (New York: Columbia University Press, 2016), 141.

13 And, furthermore, the disastrous (both politically and environmentally) mining of this stone, as delicately revealed by Judy Price in her 2014 film *White Oil*.

14 Roland Barthes, *Camera Lucida: Reflections on Photography* (New York: Hill and Wang, 2010), 29.

15 Ibid.

16 Brecht was referring to Albert Renger-Patzsch's 1928 photographs of the Fagus Factory in Alfeld, Germany, designed by Walter Gropius. See, for example, Benjamin H.D. Buchloh, "Thomas Struth's Archive," *Thomas Struth: Photographs*, exh. cat. (Chicago: Renaissance Society at the University of Chicago, 1990), 8.

17 Owen Hatherley, “Photography and Modern Architecture,” *The Photographers' Gallery Blog*, December 10, 2012, https://thephotographersgalleryblog.org.uk/2012/12/10/photoarchitecture1/.

18 David Campany, “Architecture as Photography: Document, Publicity, Commentary, Art,” in *Constructing Worlds: Photography and Architecture in the Modern Age*, exh. cat., ed. Alona Pardo and Elias Redstone (London: Barbican Gallery; Munich: Prestel Verlag, 2014).

19 According to Munther Dajani, recounting his memories of the hotel.

20 Thanks to Lucie Ryzova for this point, in reference to the advent of photography in Cairo.

١٧ مقالة أوين هاذرلي عن التصوير الفوتوغرافي والعمارة الحديثة:
Owen Hatherley, "Photography and Modern Architecture," *The Photographers' Gallery Blog*, December 10, 2012, https://thephotographersgalleryblog.org.uk/2012/12/10/photoarchitecture1/.

١٨ مقالة ديفيد كامباني عن العمارة كتصوير فوتوغرافي:
David Campany, "Architecture as Photography: Document, Publicity, Commentary, Art," in *Constructing Worlds: Photography and Architecture in the Modern Age*, exh. cat., ed. Alona Pardo and Elias Redstone (London: Barbican Gallery; Munich: Prestel Verlag, 2014).

١٩ طبقاً لرواية منذر الدجاني وهو يستعيد ذكرياته المتعلقة بالفندق.

٢٠ أشكر لوسي ريزوفا (Lucie Ryzova) على إثارة هذه النقطة المتعلقة بظهور التصوير الفوتوغرافي في القاهرة.

١٠ كتب المستشار المدني لشؤون القدس تشارلز روبرت آشبي بعد الحرب العالمية الأولى «إن نبض المسلم عندما قام بالتعمير مختلف عن نبضنا، لم يفكر بالأمور ضمن هيكلية معينة أو سياسة. اختار جزئيات جميلة رقع بها نمطاً جميلاً يساعده على الحلم، ثم استراح وجعل يحلم.» مقتبس من مقالة نيكولاس روبرتس:
Nicholas E. Roberts, "Dividing Jerusalem: British Urban Planning in the Holy City," *Journal of Palestine Studies* 42, no. 4 (Summer 2013), 14.

١١ مقالة سليم تماري عن القدس كمدينة الرعاع في زمن الحرب بين عامي ١٩١٧ و ١٩٢١:
Salim Tamari, "City of Riffraff: Crowds, Public Space, and New Urban Sensibilities in War-Time Jerusalem, 1917–1921," in *Comparing Cities: The Middle East and South Asia*, ed. Kamran Asdar Ali and Martina Rieker (Oxford: Oxford University Press, 2010).

١٢ مقابلة مع سعاد العامري، أجرى المقابلة آمال أندراوس ونورا عكاوي:
Suad Amiry, "Interview with Suad Amiry," in *The Arab City: Architecture and Representation*, ed. Amale Andraos and Nora Akawi (New York: Columbia University Press, 2016), 141.

١٣ إضافة إلى ذلك، قطع الحجر من الكسارات، وهو أمر كارثي على المستويين السياسي والبيئي، كما نرى في فيلم جودي برايس White Oil — إنتاج عام ٢٠١٤.

١٤ كتاب رولاند بارت:
Roland Barthes, *Camera Lucida: Reflections on Photography* (New York: Hill and Wang, 2010), 29.

١٥ المصدر السابق.

١٦ كان بريشت يشير إلى صور فوتوغرافية للمصور ألبرت رينغر-باتزش من عام ١٩٢٨، لمصنع ڤاغوس في آلفلد بألمانيا والذي صممه والتر غروبيوس. انظر مثلاً:
Benjamin H.D. Buchloh, "Thomas Struth's Archive," *Thomas Struth: Photographs*, exh. cat. (Chicago: Renaissance Society at the University of Chicago, 1990), 8.

بالإمكان أن يسعها كوخ العائلة المقبب، لذا قاموا ببناء هيكل أكبر له، وقد ظلت القبة تتهاوى فيه كل الوقت. وعندما نجحوا أخيراً، كان داخل الكوخ معتماً فلم يستطع التصوير. انتهى الأمر بأن اضطر نانوك وعائلته أن يعيشوا في كوخ جليدي من ثلاثة جوانب فقط، وبقي الجانب الأخير مفتوحاً من أجل الكاميرا: حتى تساعدنا على تخيل فضاءاتهم الداخلية. جاءت طريقتي في رواية الحداثة الفلسطينية شبيهة بهذا؛ تنهار القصة بمجرد أن أحاول تمثيلها بسلاسة.

أتطلع إلى رؤيتك،

عريب

رأيت رجالاً منشغلين بحوارات جدية وهم جالسون على البار ونساء في فساتين جميلة للسهرة. جمعت صوراً في مجموعة واحدة وطلبت أن آخذها إلى الكلية حتى يطلع عليها طلابي الذين يعملون على مشاريع حول هذا المبنى. أصر واحد من الأخوة أن أعود في اليوم التالي، حتى يتسنى لهم عدّ الصور وترتيبها. عندما عدت في اليوم التالي وجدت أن مجموعة الصور قد تحولت إلى صور شخصيات دينية في مؤتمرات رسمية في قاعة الاحتفالات وصور نوادل يتحركون بين الطاولات وصور عائلات سعيدة. ربما كان هذا المسح عملية حاسمة. ربما فهموا أن الطلاب سينشرون الصور على مواقع التواصل الاجتماعي مع تعليقات صاخبة، «انظروا، كنا فيما مضى حداثيون!»

يا ترى أين تبدأ «الحداثة» بالنسبة لك في عملك؟ هل لها فعلاً ساعة محددة، مثل ساعة الإصباح بعد العتمة؟ دائماً متأخرة؟[٢٠] هناك تمثيل رائع في بالي للفيلم الصامت «نانوك الشمال»، من إخراج روبرت ج. فلاهرتي عام ١٩٢٢، والذي أراد أن يوثق حياة عائلة من الأسكيمو. كانت مشكلته أن كاميرته لم يكن

لطالما كان التصوير الفوتوغرافي شيئاً ذا حدين وموضوعه العمارة. كتب أوين هاذرلي عن العمارة الحديثة أنها بدأت تتجاوب مع الصور التي توثقها بأن أصبحت أكثر جمالاً في الصور، وأن ظهور الأفلام الملونة كان له تأثير في إضافة الألوان وكذلك درجات اللون الواحد إلى واجهات المباني.[١٧] في هذه الأثناء، بنى داڤيد كامباني على توكيدات ڤالتر بنيامين أن «نوع الفن (والعمارة) التي ستنتصر في النهاية ستكون تلك التي تبدو جيدة في الصور الفوتوغرافية»، واقترح أن القيمة الثقافية للعمارة تخترعها صورتها التي تلتقطها الكاميرا.[١٨]

إذا ما وضعنا القيمة الخارجية على جهة، يبدو أننا اخترنا أن نغير العوالم الداخلية لهذه المباني والقصص التي روتها فيما مضى. قبل ثلاث سنوات، سهرت حتى منتصف الليل مع عائلة غوشة، أنظر إلى صور فندق هيلتون كارلتون الذي أسسه والدهم الراحل د. محمد غوشة بين رام الله والقدس. أتذكر أني رأيت صور راقصات جئن من كازينو لبنان على حلبة الرقص الأولى من نوعها في المدينة، وهناك ربما غنت بيتولا كلارك «Colour My World».[١٩]

منها عنواناً فلسوف أكتب «ڤيلا كنعان» و«ڤيلا العالول» و«ڤيلا القطب» و«ڤيلا السلطي» و«ڤيلا ميخائيل»، إلخ... ما هو السياق الذي سيشرح هذا الهوس المعماري بالڤيلا؟ متى بدأت ثقافة الاستهلاك تنصب سكنى العائلة الواحدة نموذجاً لهجر المدينة القديمة بالقدس أو نابلس؟ واضح أني لم أنسَ أثر الحرب والصراع الاستعماري، وأن انتهى المطاف بمعماري البلدية من أمثال هاني عرفات بتاريخ مهني متقطع جراء قضائهم وقتاً في السجن أو ممنوعين من العودة إلى مدنهم عند رجوعهم من بعض الأسفار. كذلك لم أنسَ أن مشاريع الاستقلال حول العالم وفرت للمعماريين تمويلاً مالياً يعينهم على التجربة في بناء الملاعب والإسكانات العامة والمتاحف والمستشفيات والمكتبات، ناهيك عن المعماريين الأوروبيين الذين استطاعوا أخيراً أن يواجهوا المستقبل بعد الحرب العالمية الثانية. لكن عندما حدث التجريب عندنا، بدا أنه حدث في تصميم الفنادق والبيوت الخاصة المنفصلة التي سكنتها عائلة منفردة، وفقط في فترة «الهدوء» (أو «الراحة»، والتي ستتكرر في عمّان بعد حرب ١٩٦٧).

الذي يخترقنا كسهم ويساعدنا أن نفهم موقعها ونقرأها: «المصور الفوتوغرافي يعلمني ماذا يرتدي الروس».[١٤] يصبح المرء وراء العدسة فجأة مخبراً عليه أن يوفر شكل من أشكال «التعليم» للمتفرج الذي يقلب بين الصفحات ليتخيل مكاناً: «أرى طاقية الولد القماشية الكبيرة وربطة عنق ولد آخر.»[١٥] أصبح الفلسطيني اللاجئ، على الأخص، الموضوع المفضل للكاميرا التي تصور مكاناً متخيلاً من خلال صور هذا المكان نفسه. ماذا كان سيحدث لو أنا أزلنا الناس من الصورة، من الإشارة؟ ليس الشيء نفسه، المكان، وإنما المؤشر، صورته الفوتوغرافية التي هربت، فرّغت، وتبدلت جزئياً.

فكرة برتولت بريشت عن الصورة الفوتوغرافية المشهورة لمصنع تخبرنا قليلاً عما يحدث داخل ذلك المصنع.[١٦] لا تخبرنا الصورة عن الطبقة الاجتماعية ولا العلاقات العمالية التي تشكل هذا النظام الذي نراه فيما تمثله الصورة. الحقيقة أني أيضاً انتهيت إلى صور فردية ومسطحة وأمامية، منزوعة الأشخاص لواجهات معمارية، وبخاصة لتلك الأيقونة المرتبطة بجوهر البرجوازية: الفيلا. لو كنت سأعطي كل واحدة

وموجة المبشرين الأمريكان الذين جاءوا عكس تلك الرحلة. مر على الفترة التي أهتم بها بصفحة واحدة من عرضه على الباوربوينت، أعطاها عنوان «الخمسينيات والستينيات». كثيراً ما أفكر في هذه الـ«ات»، وكأنها تشير إلى تعدد السنوات. لمَ تبدو كتسجيل بين حربين تحت الحكم الأردني يتلعثم كل مرة أردنا أن نسمعه؟ لمَ تعتقد أن هذه الفترة لا يمكن سماعها؟

أحب أن أعرف ماذا يعني لك وأنت مؤرخ اجتماعي، تثري معرفتك في أقبية الأرشيف الغريبة وتبحث في الأرقام المدهشة العصية على التصديق والمرتبطة بالمدينة الفلسطينية الحديثة، وأنا مستمرة في أخذ صوري دون أي أشخاص فيها. يبدو جلياً أن كثيراً من هذه المباني قد فرّغتها الحرب والهجرة من أهلها. وفي بعض الحالات، رغم ذلك، أتعمد إزالة الأشخاص الذين يبقون في محيط صورة مشهدي. عندي إحساس بأن عليّ أن أستثني كل صورة يظهرون بها أو أن أغير توجيه عدستي فلا أعود أراهم. كان أقل أعمال رولاند بارت إثارة نظريته الضخمة عن «ملعب» الصورة الفوتوغرافية، والعنصر

حتى يضع لها مخططاً أساسياً. في غضون شهرين، قدم ماكلين بأعجوبة مجموعة من السياسات التي لا تزال تتحكم بنمط البناء في جزء كبير من البيئة المبينة فيما يعرف اليوم باسم «فلسطين المحتلة»، أو ما تسميه سعاد العامري «فلسطين الصغرى» (الضفة الغربية والقدس الشرقية وقطاع غزة).[١٢] أطول هذه القوانين والأنظمة عمراً هو القانون الذي يحتم أن تكون واجهات المباني في الضفة الغربية والقدس مبنية «بحجر محلي». حتى بعدما تحول الحجر من عنصر بناء إلى عنصر زينة؛ غطاء لطوب خرساني مفرغ وفولاذ، قشرة من حجر رقيق، مستخرج من الكسارات، مقصوص على الآلات، ومدهون باللون الأبيض.[١٣]

في نفس المؤتمر، تجاوز محاضر آخر، يزيد الرفاعي، كل الفترة من ١٩٤٨ حتى وصل زمن «الفياضية» عام ٢٠٠٧، عندما أتاح تشريع القروض البنكية تحت إدارة رئيس الوزراء سلام فياض الطفرة العقارية الحالية في رام الله. رسم المحاضر بقصص رائعة الموجة الأولى من هجرات الفلسطينيين الأولى من رام الله إلى الأمريكيتين في القرن التاسع عشر،

عزيزي سليم،

هذي صورة كنت أبحث عنها في هاتفي عندما أخبرتك بأنني أتذكر محاضرتك في رام الله في تموز ٢٠١٥ عن القدس كـ«مدينة مخللة». كنت قد رسمت صورة مذهلة في ذهني عن موظفي الانتداب البريطاني (ماكلين وآشبي وستورز) وهم يمشون في القدس، ويشتكون من رائحة «نتنة»، وهم يقيسون جوانبها، بغية المحافظة عليها مثل أي مقتنى متحفي.[١٠] أفكر في هذه الشخصيات كل يوم وأنا هنا في أكسفورد؛ اثنان اثنان، يحملان أمتارهما ودفاترهما، ويذرعان ساحات الكلية يملآن نماذجهما. رجال يلبسون الأسود، ودائماً كثنائيات.

عندما قدمت نسخة من عملي «مواد لكتاب عن حداثات فلسطينية» في غلاسكو، علمت أن السير ويليام ماكلين كان عضواً في الحزب الوحدوي الاسكتلندي. كما شرحت في مقالتك :«مدينة الرعاع»، ماكلين كان مهندس مدن يعمل في المكتب الاستعماري البريطاني.[١١] استدعي عام ١٩١٨ من عمله كمهندس مدن في الاسكندرية لزيارة مدينة القدس

Blue Sky Thinking

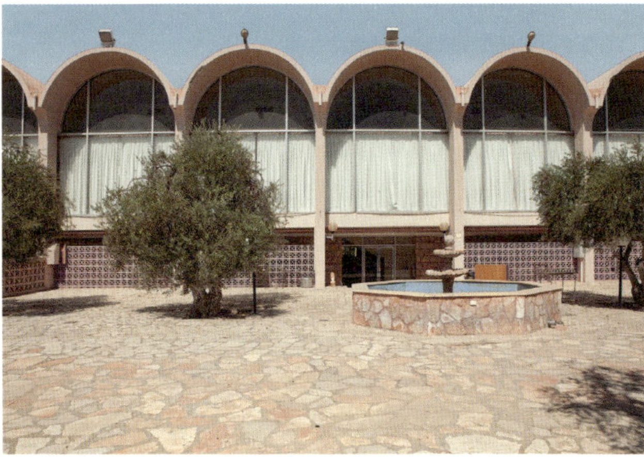

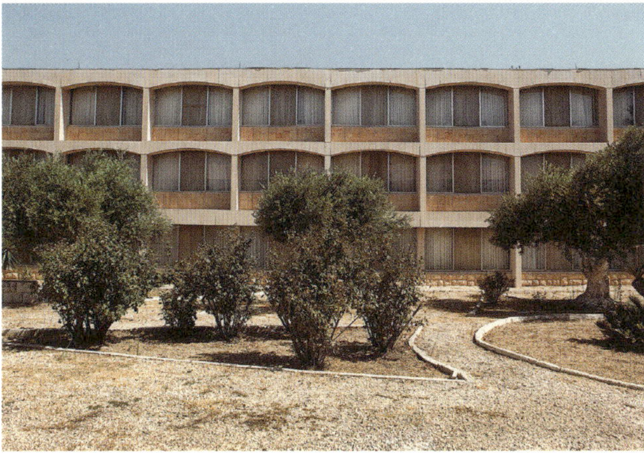

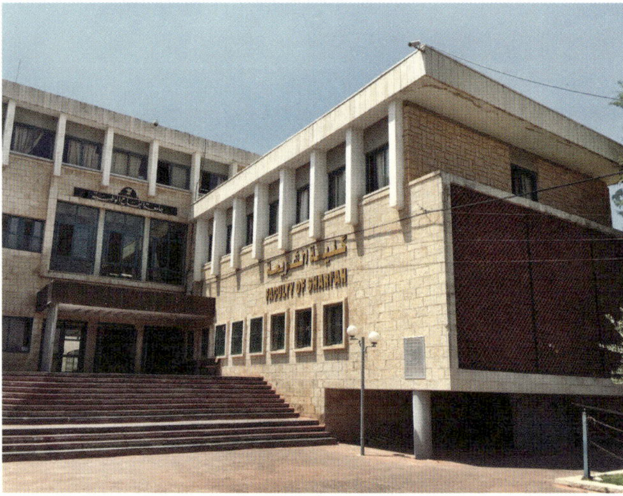
FACULTY OF SHARIAH

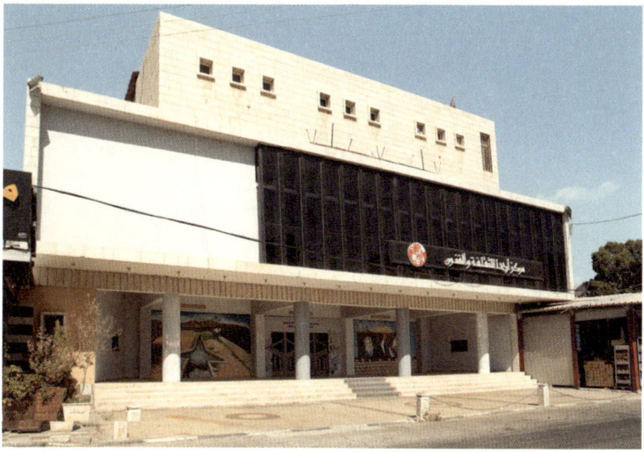

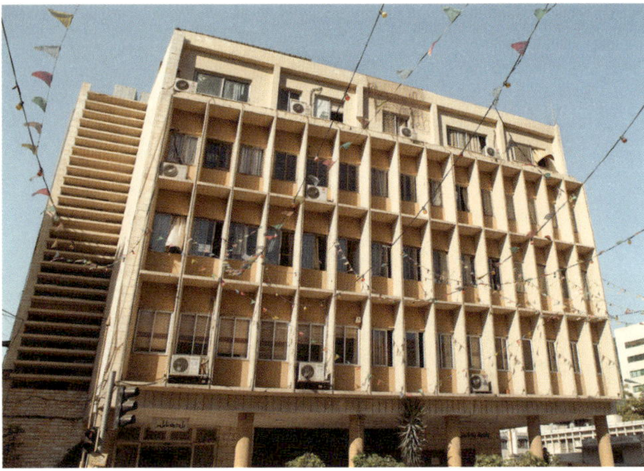

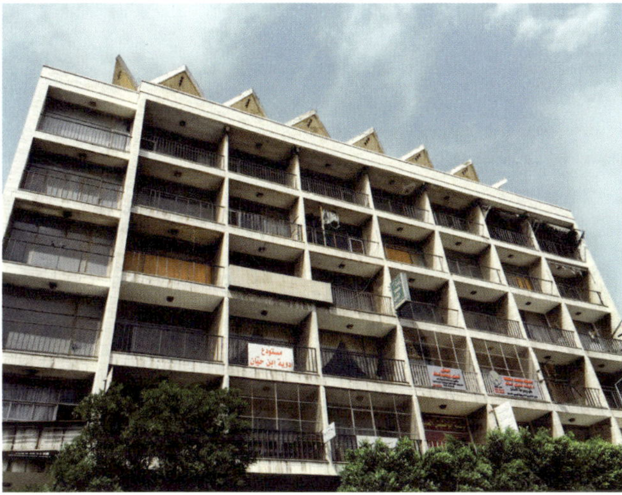
مستودع
دوية ابن حيّان

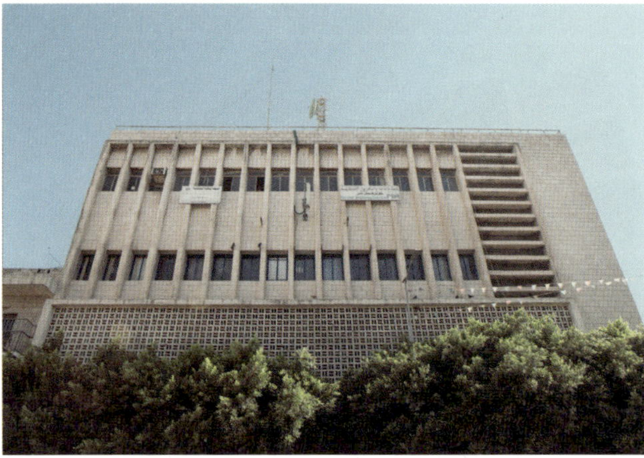

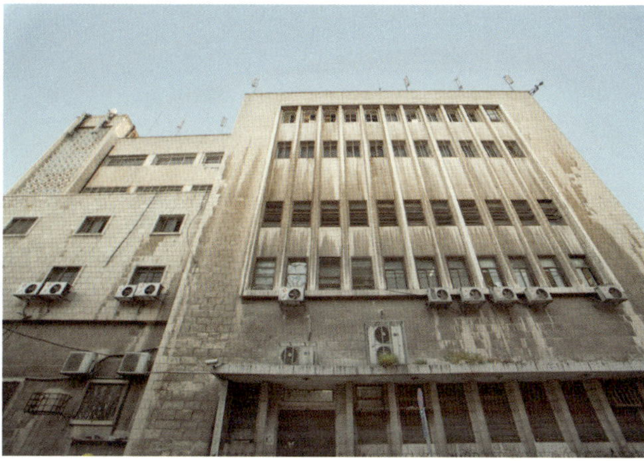

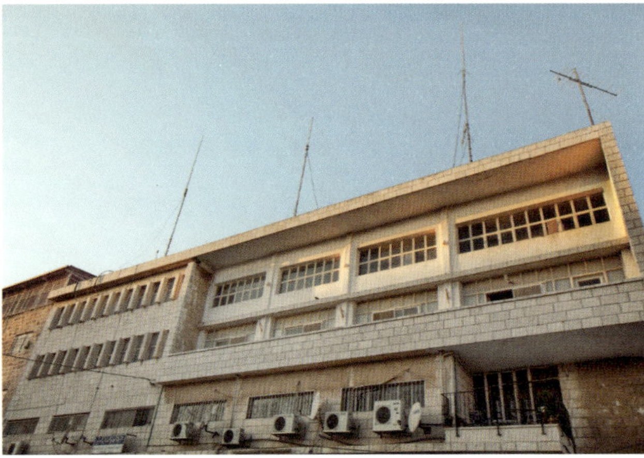

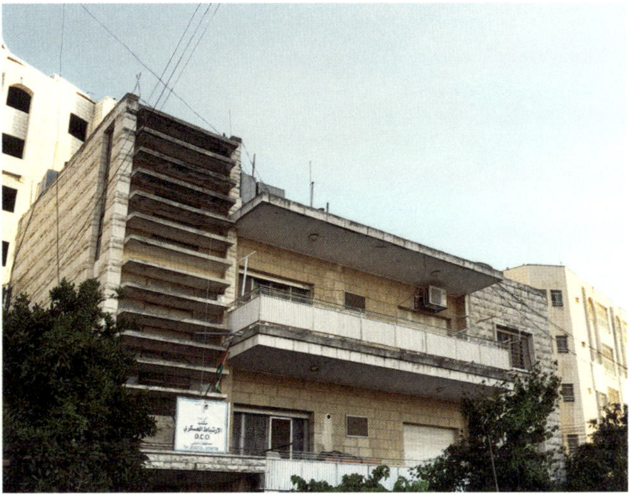
الارتباط العسكري
D.C.O

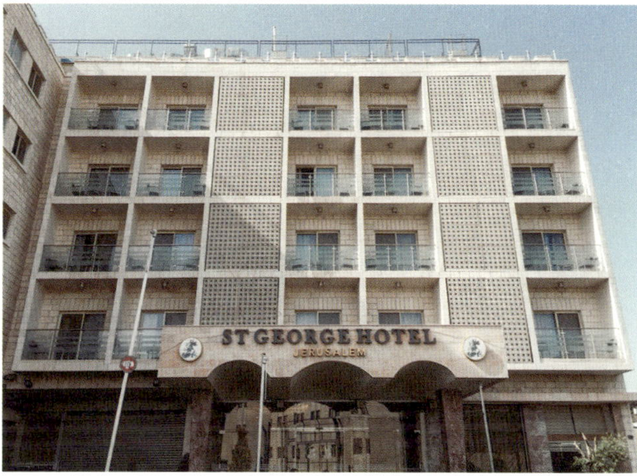
ST GEORGE HOTEL
JERUSALEM

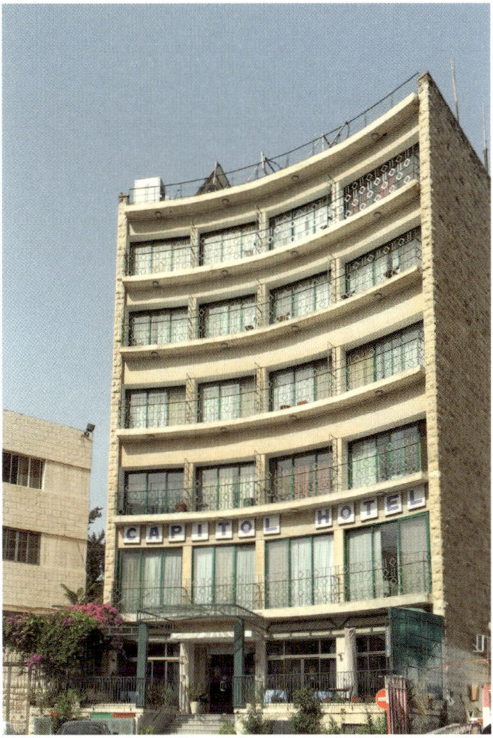
CAPITOL HOTEL

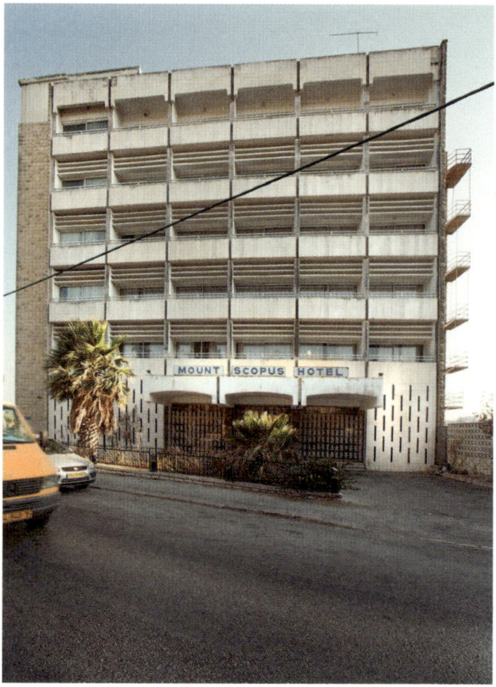
MOUNT SCOPUS HOTEL

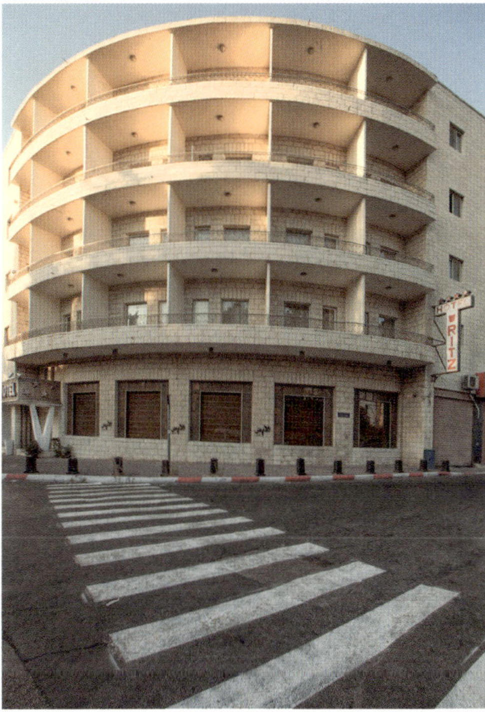
RITZ

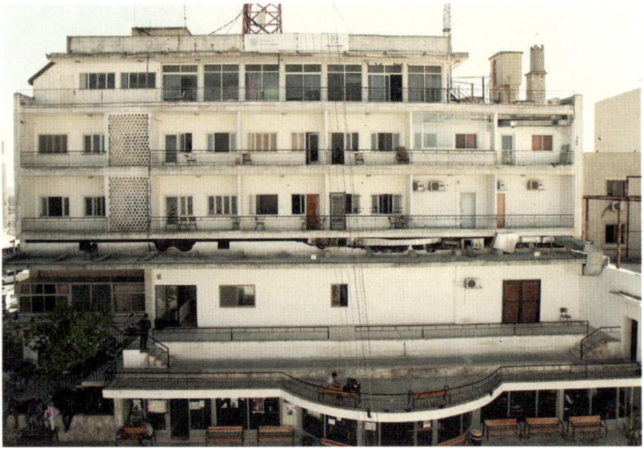

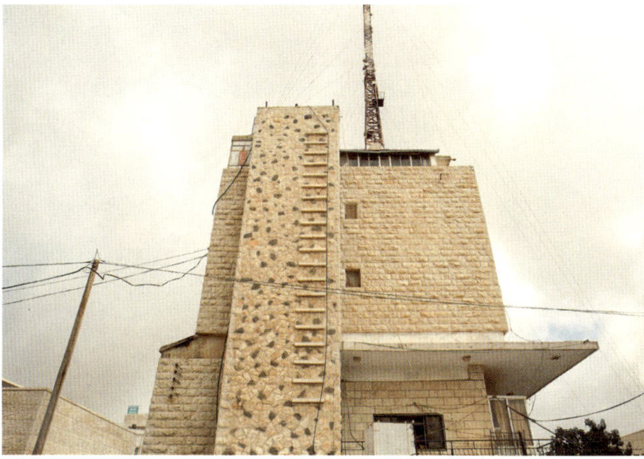

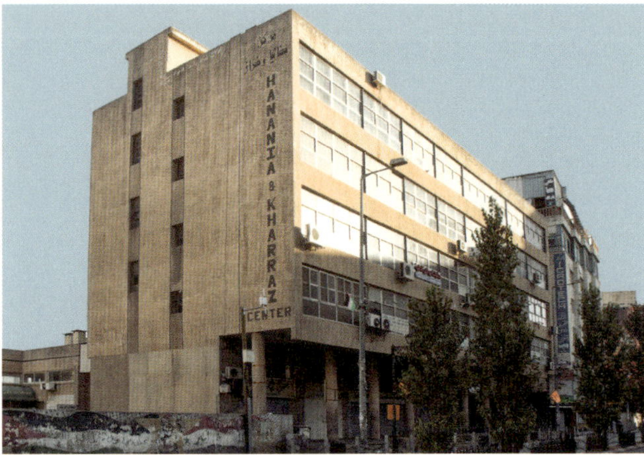
HANANIA & KHARRAZ
CENTER

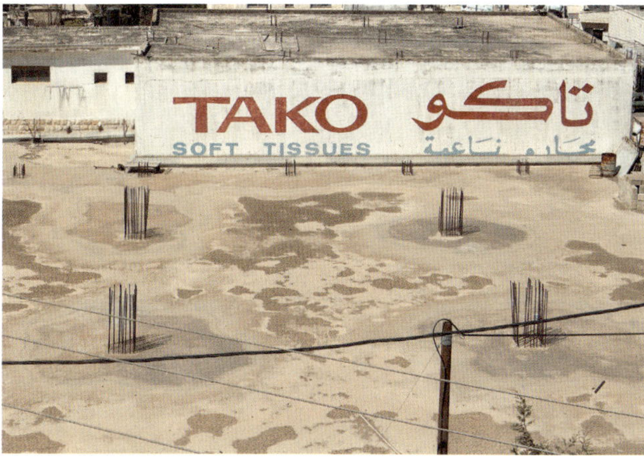
TAKO
SOFT TISSUES
تاكو
محارم ناعمة

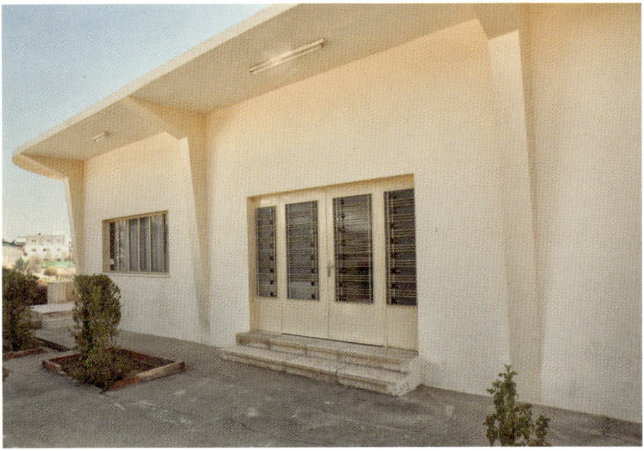

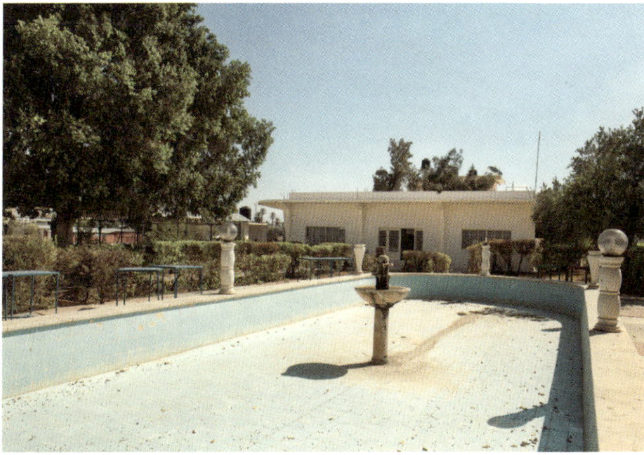

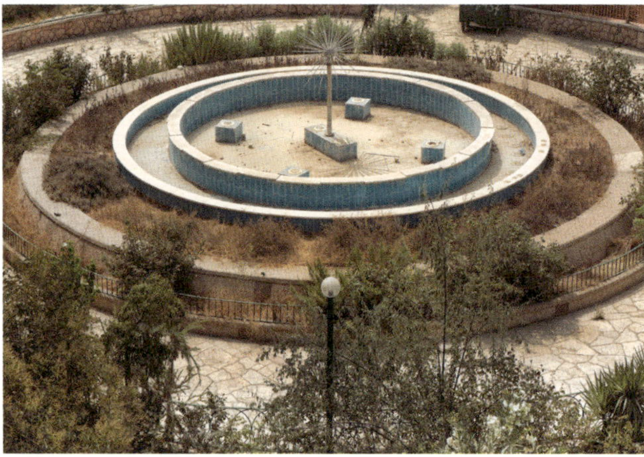

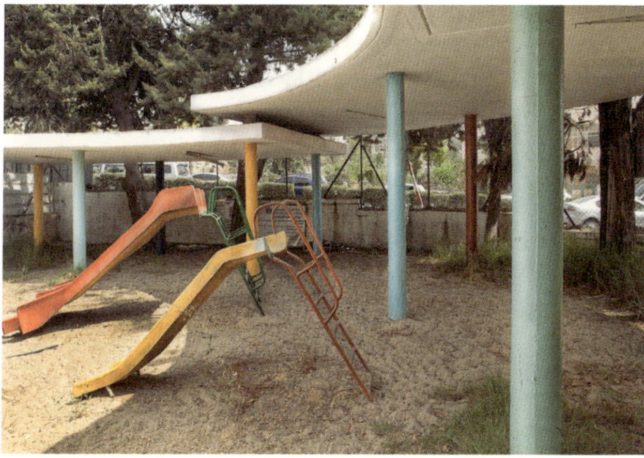

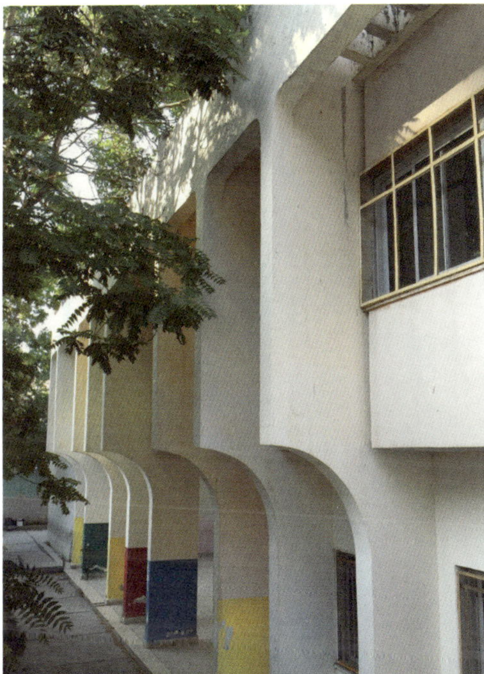

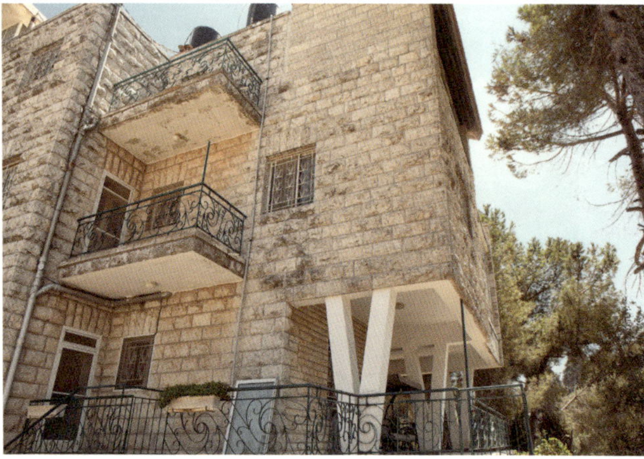

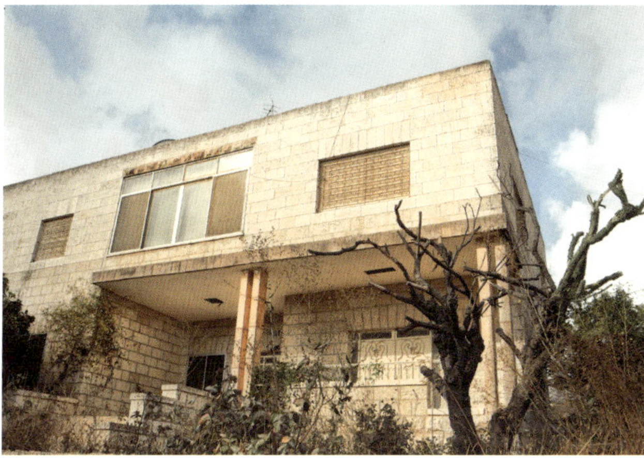

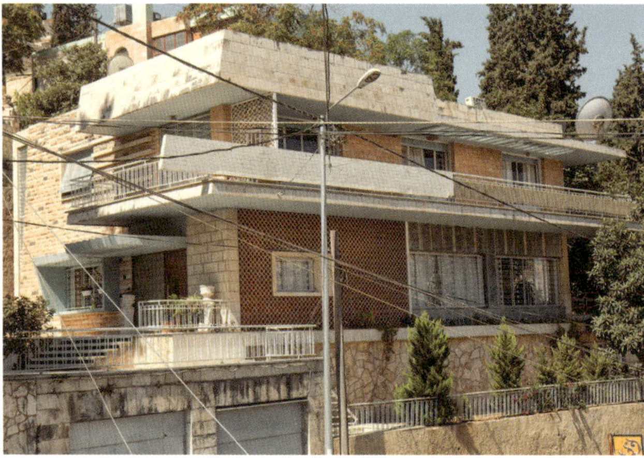

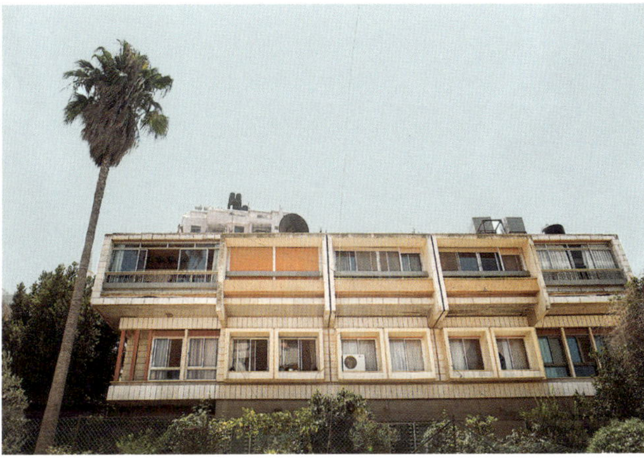

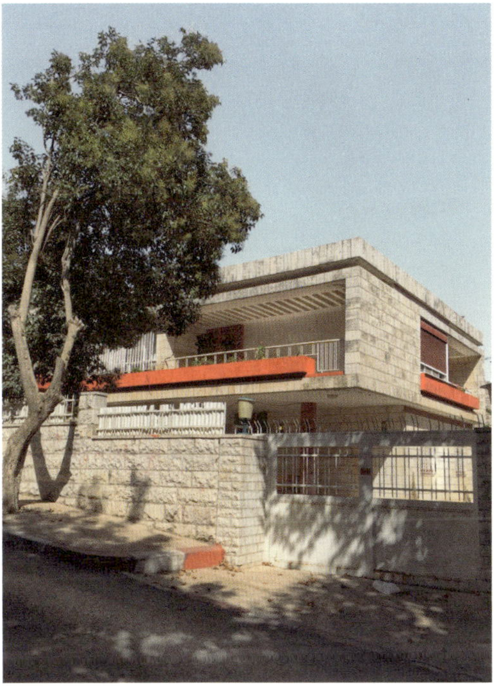

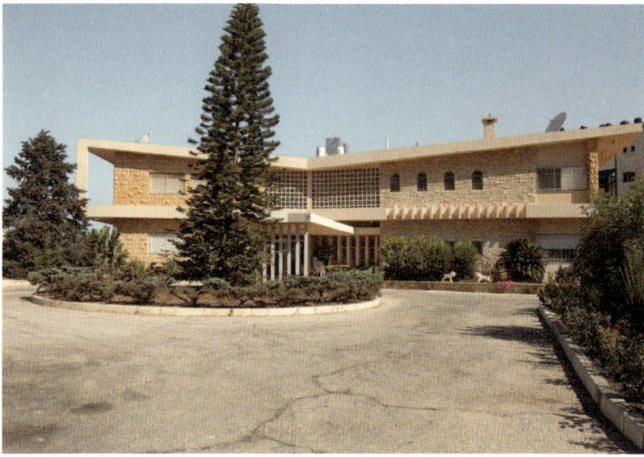

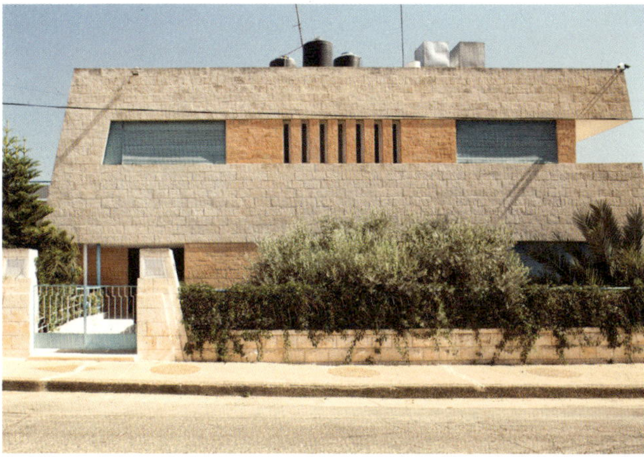

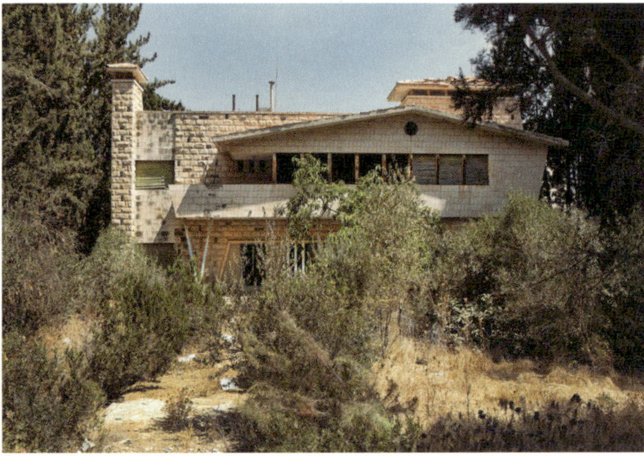

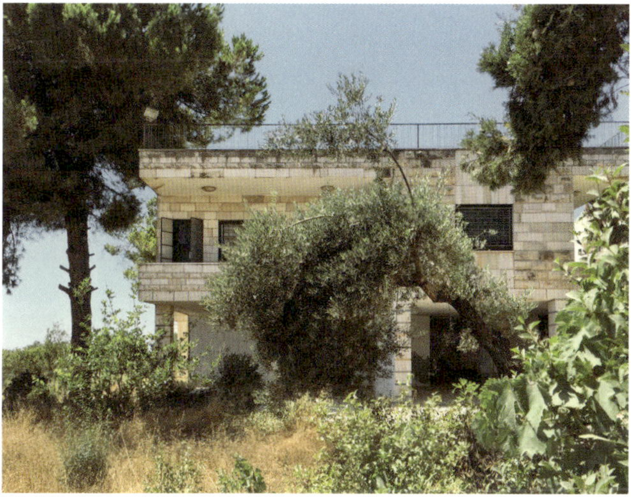

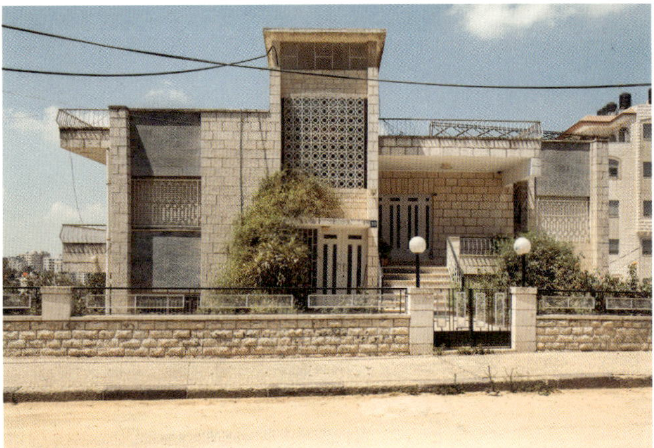

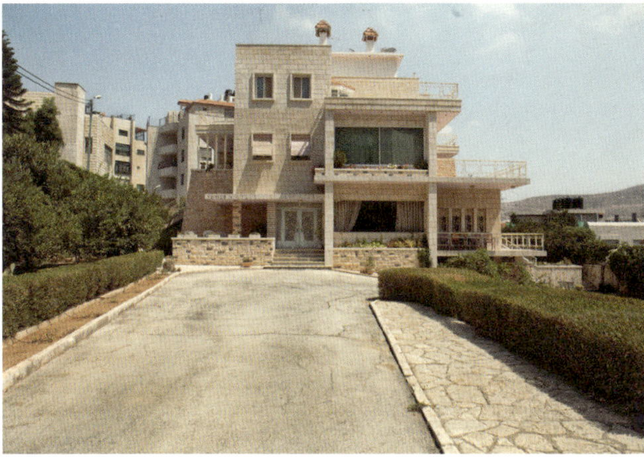

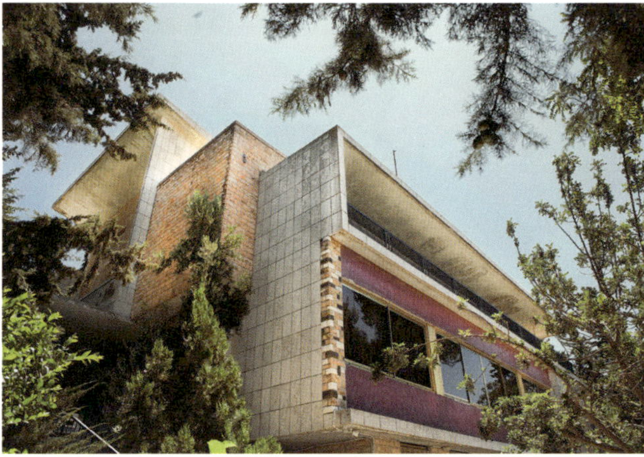

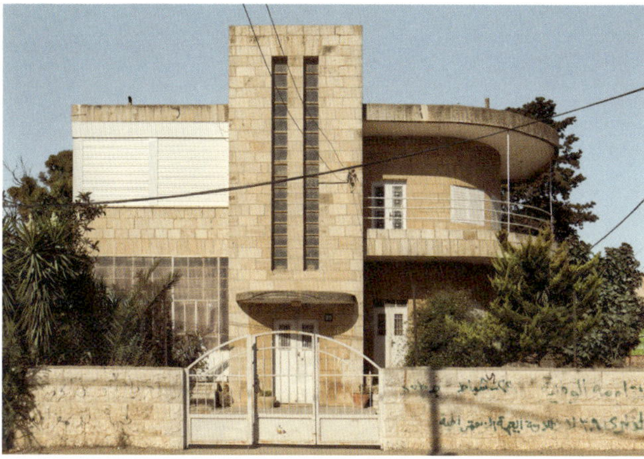

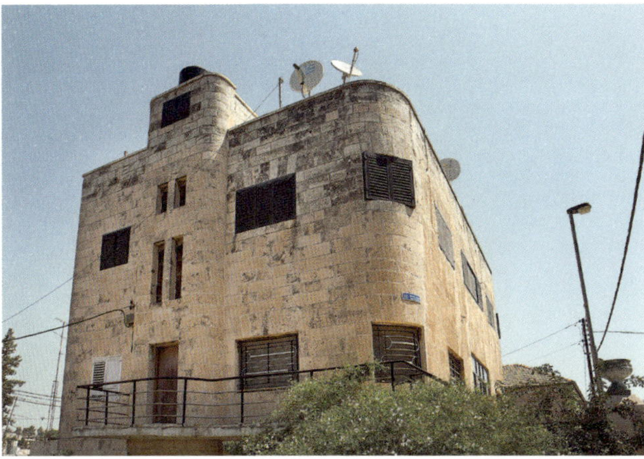

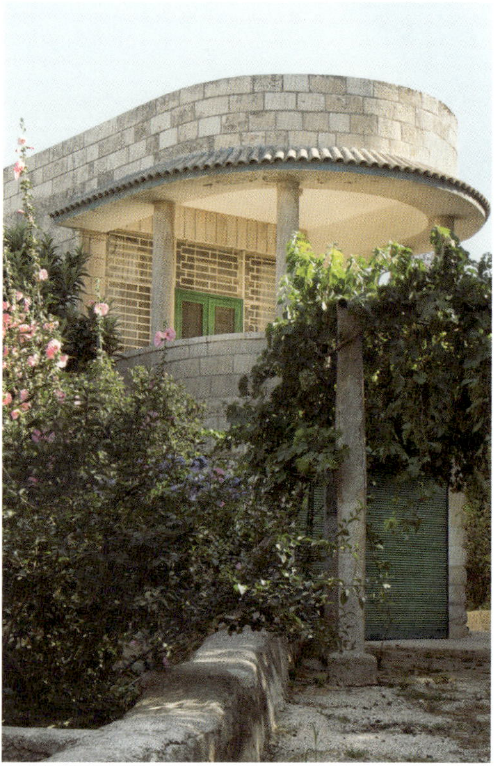

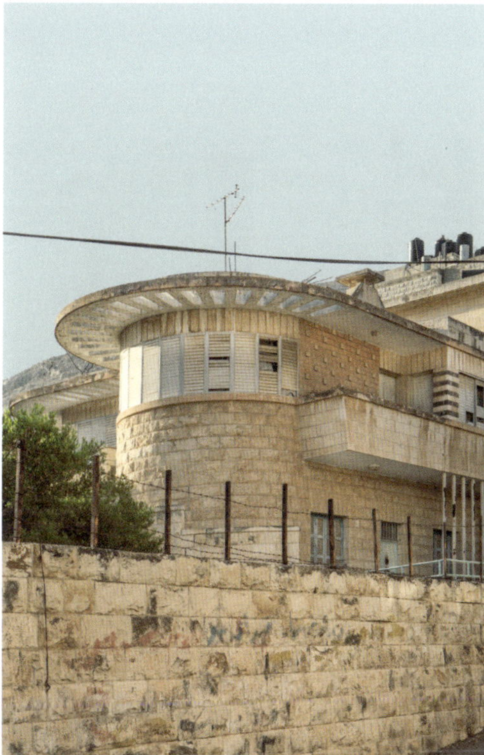

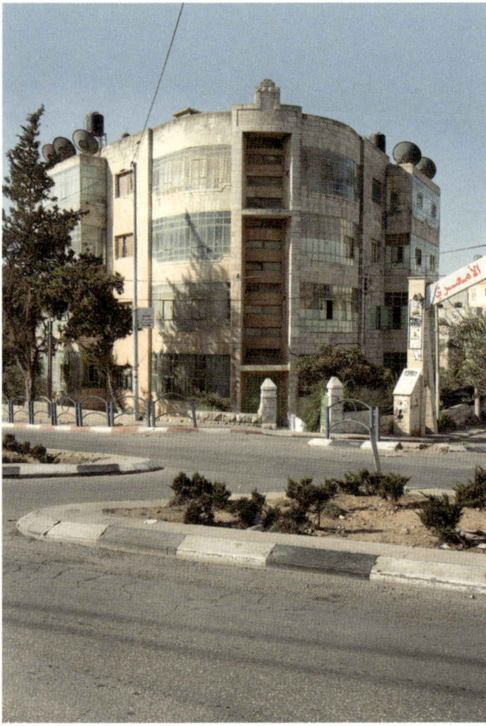

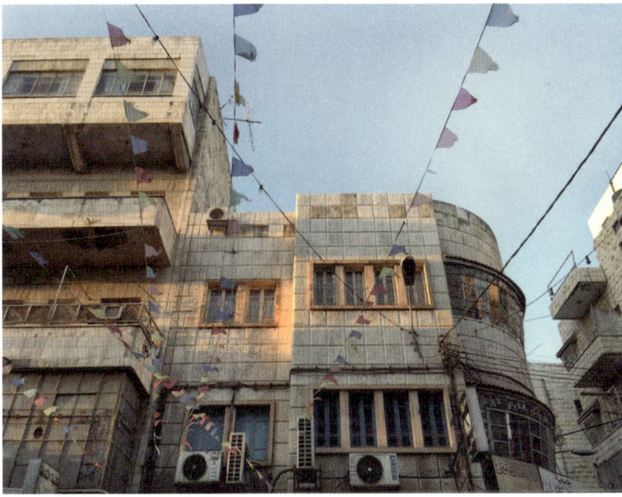

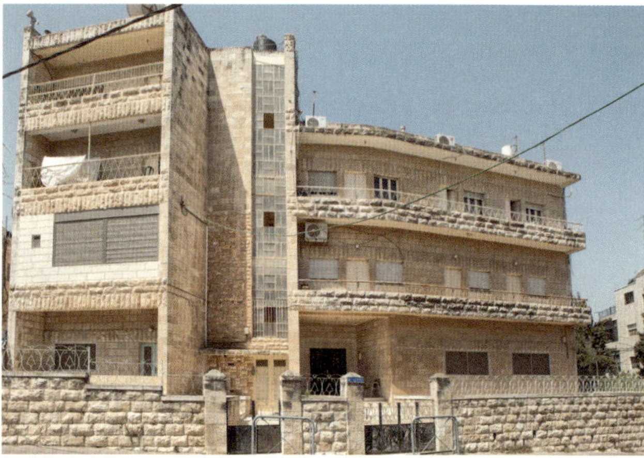

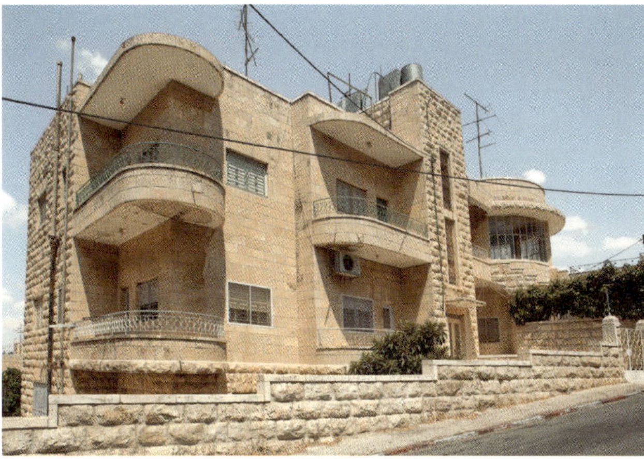

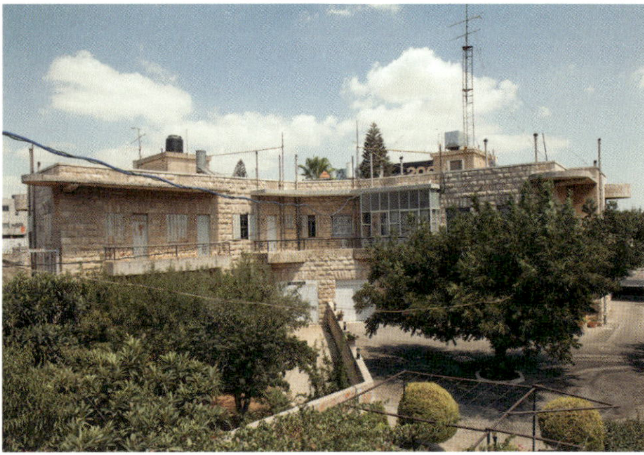

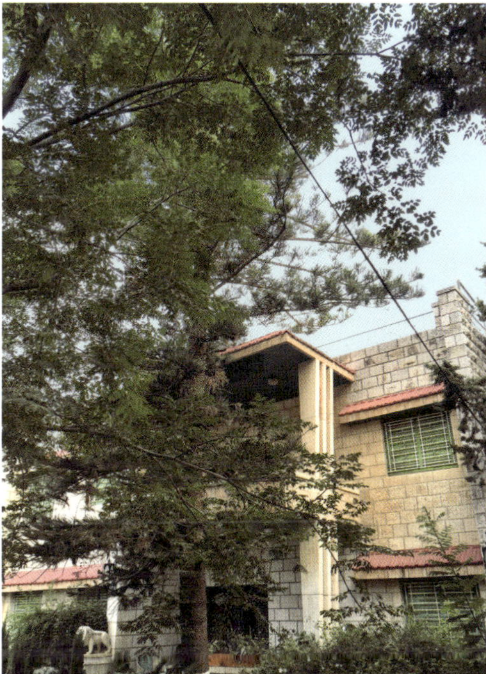

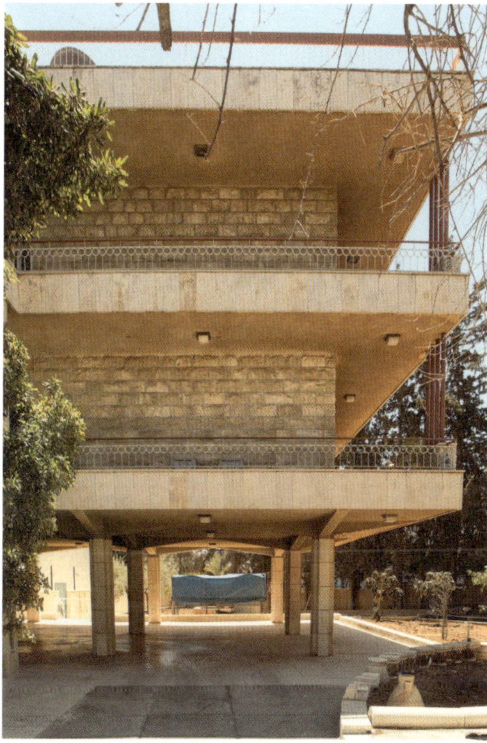

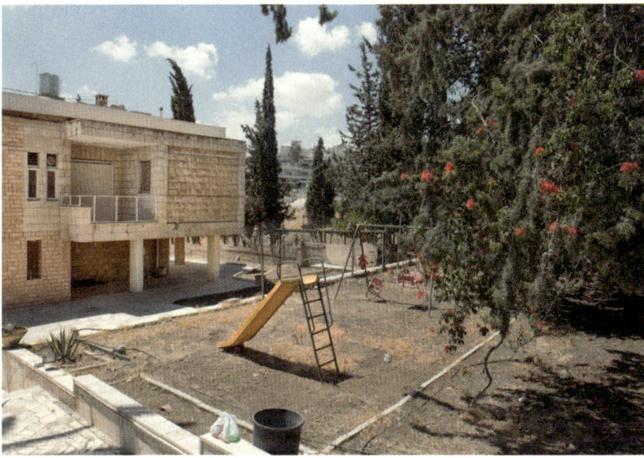

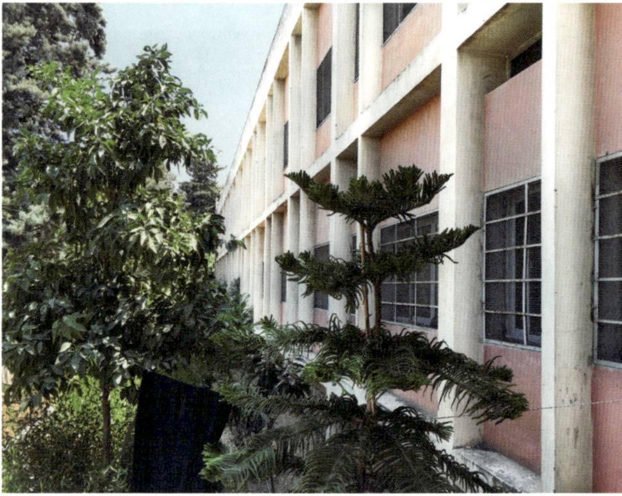

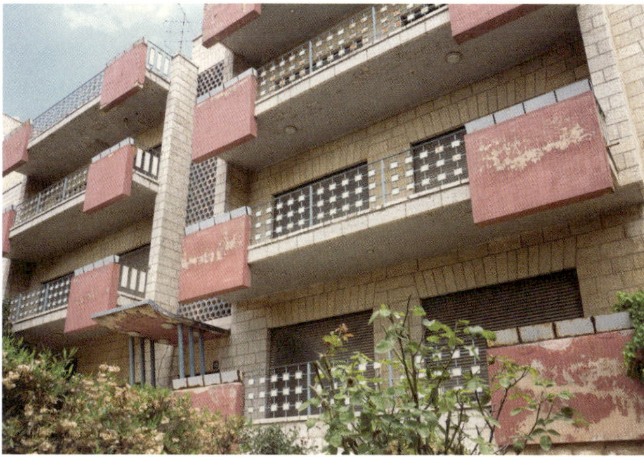

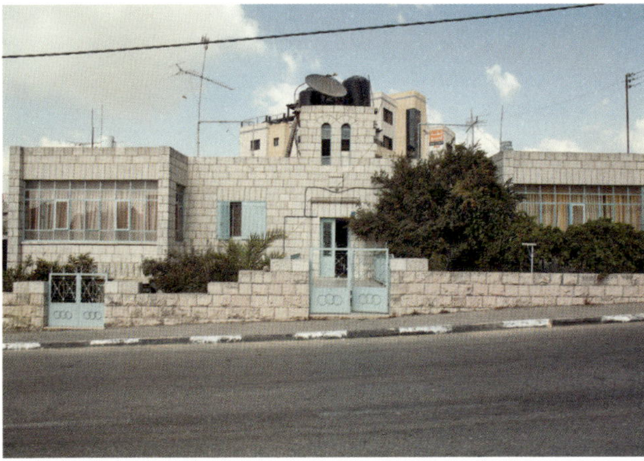

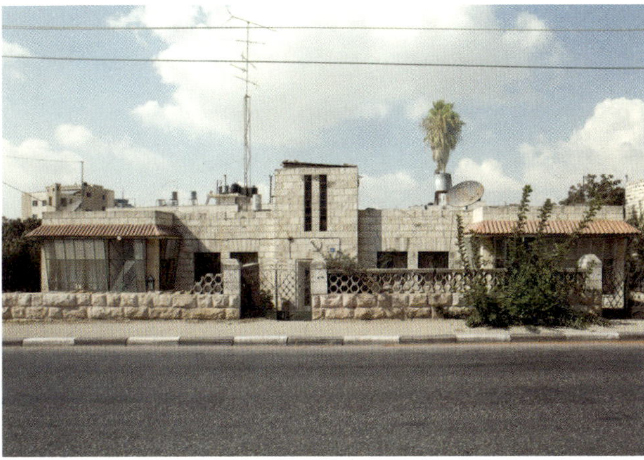

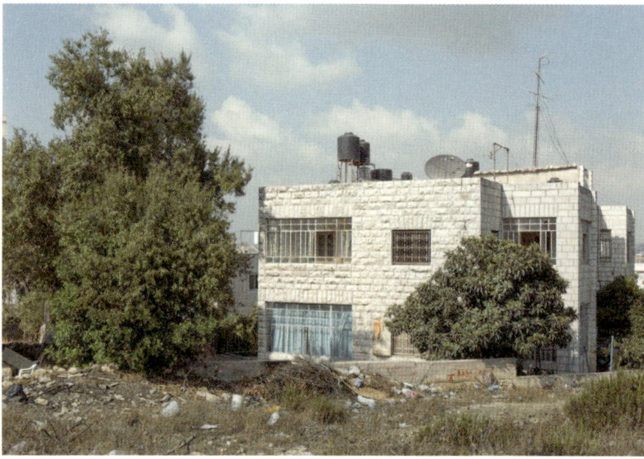

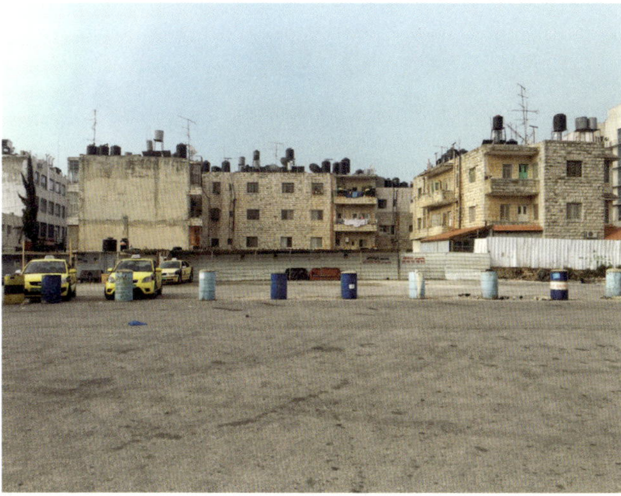

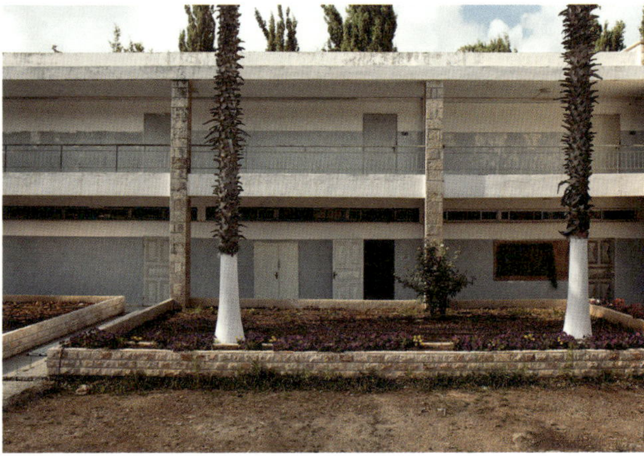

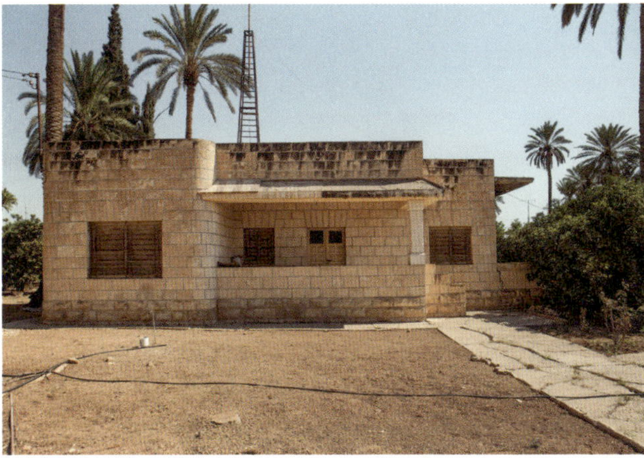

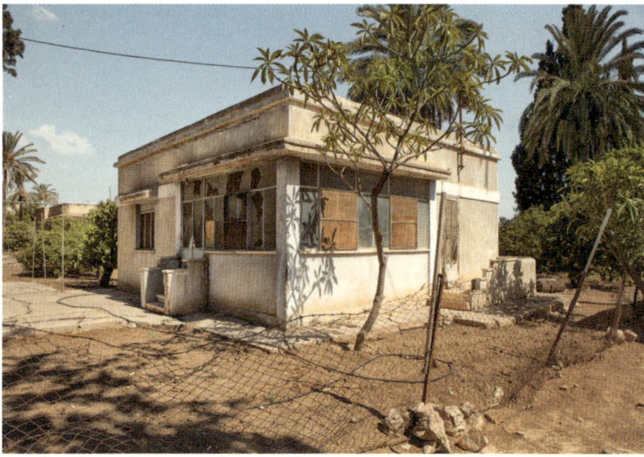

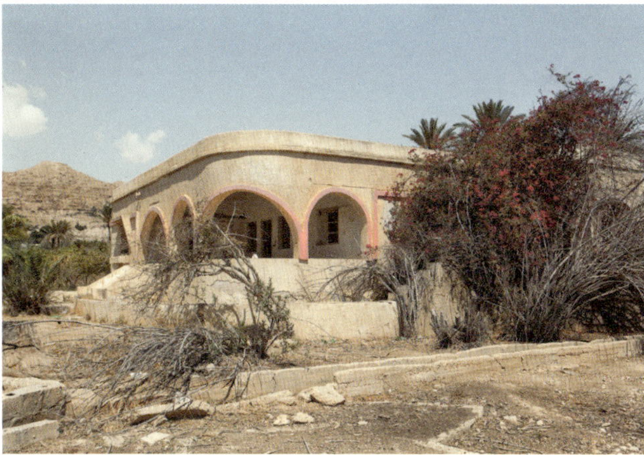

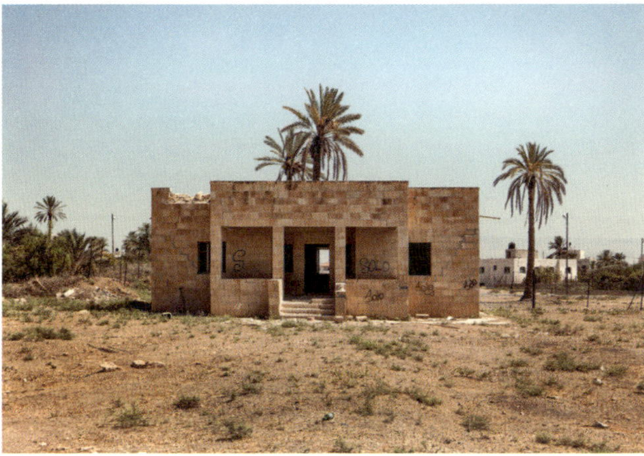

طبقة من المظاهر

Hani Arafat,
The Color of Sun

I wanted to take a proper photograph of one of Hani Arafat's buildings with a fancy camera. I brought one with me the next time I was in Nablus, in order to photograph his building on the An-Najah National University campus. I was stopped by security as I was going through the gate. I said that I wished to take a photo of the main university building. The two guards turned around and looked at the building. "Go ahead," said one of them. "What is it for?" asked the other. "I like it," I said. "Well, then you need to get clearance from the PR office before you go in." The first guard, the more laid-back one, called the office, explained the situation, and spent a while listening and nodding his head before he hung up the phone. "I'm sorry," he said, "I spoke too soon. You need to call the vice president in person and explain." He dialed the extension, I took the warm receiver from his hand; a woman answered. "Hello?" "Hi, my name is Oraib Toukan. I am an artist and I am interested in the work of architect Hani Arafat, who built a building in your university in the early '60s. I would love to take a photograph of it." "You will need to speak directly to the vice president about this, my dear," she said, "I will go ahead and transfer you."

"Hi, my name is Oraib Toukan. I head the media studies program at Al-Quds University. I simply wish to take one photograph, and it's of the main building of An-Najah University," I explained again. "You are calling from the gate, yes?" the vice president asked. "Yes," I replied. "Please come in for tea and introduce yourself. I will need to get permission. My secretary explained that you have been transferred a few times. I am really sorry that it has been so complicated!" I walked up to his office to have tea. I found him interesting,

and we chatted a little about Brandeis University's withdrawal of support from Al-Quds University because the former were horrified by a Twitter image of a Palestinian Islamic Jihad student rally on campus.
He called his boss, explained my request, listened to a long answer, and hung up. "I am terribly sorry, you can't take a photograph after all." I asked why—in retrospect I feel I was a little rude in tone, and I am still upset at myself. "A section of the building you are interested in is now the Department of Shari'ah [religious studies]. The Israeli army loves any excuse to raid our universities. We really don't need more attention," he said to me. I thanked him for his time and walked out. Outside, I took out a smartphone from my purse, zoomed in, and took a shot. I noticed a bust on a plinth right next to the short, circular concrete pillars holding the more modular structure of Hani Arafat's

building. I approached it and saw that it was a bust of one of the founders of the university: mathematician, theorist, and activist Qadri Toukan.

Hani Arafat's works reveal themselves very, very slowly. They appear as one thing, and develop into another. Always seemingly foldable, raw, and colored with various stones (*m'sam sam*, *tubzi*, *ahmar majli*). But then they transform once again when you encounter their cubical mass from the other side.

Arafat received his degree in architecture from Cairo University in 1955 and began working in Kuwait, then Amman in the Department of Public Works, alongside his private practice, before joining the Nablus Municipality as chief architect. Like a number of architects at the time, he was, without question, part of the civil independence movement, which resulted in a brief period of exile. His daughter, the incredibly energetic Nablus-based architect Reema Arafat showed me the following drawings of his realized and unrealized works.

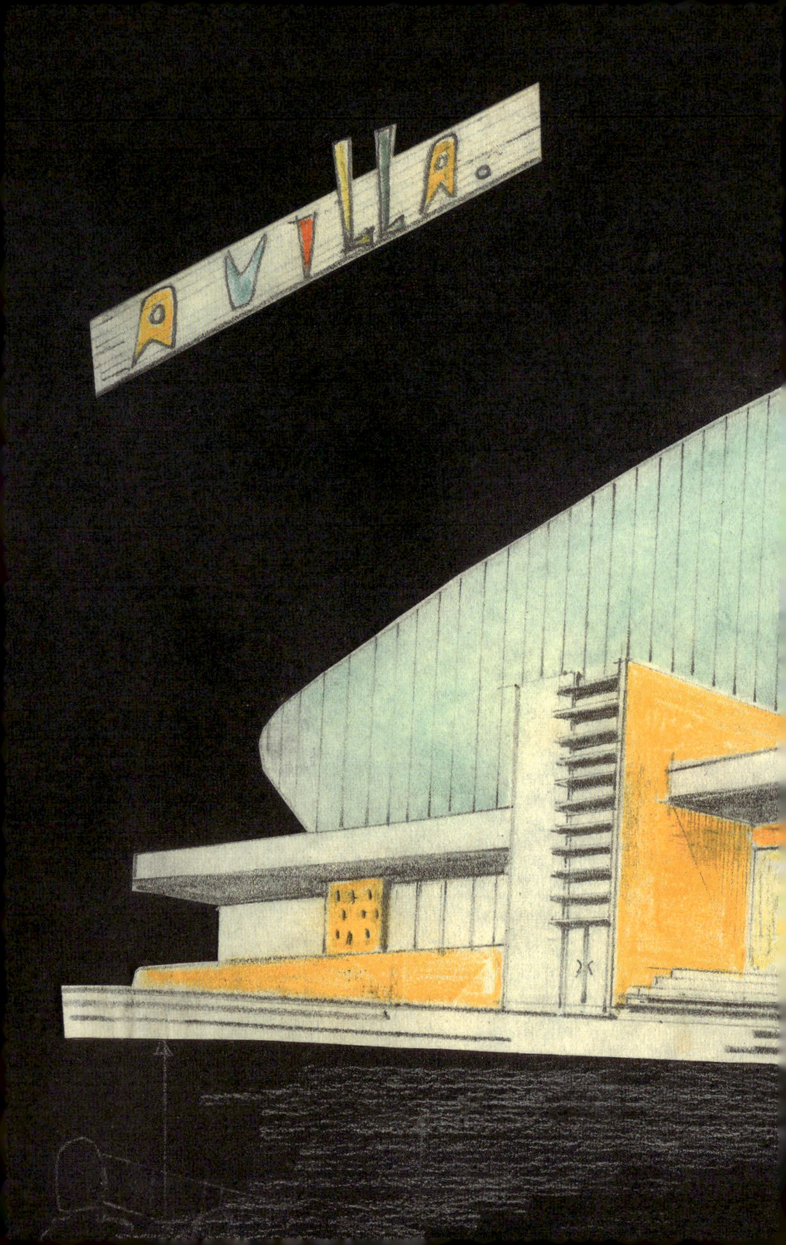
AVILLA.

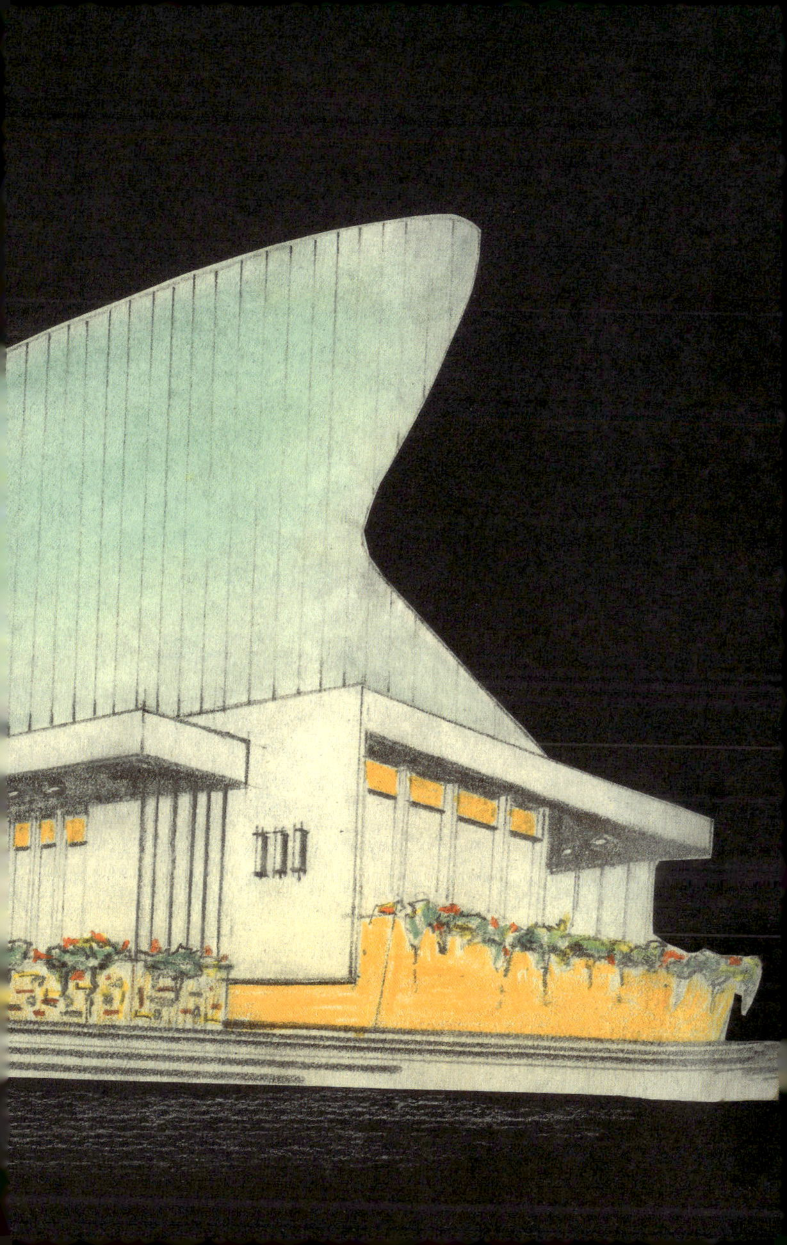

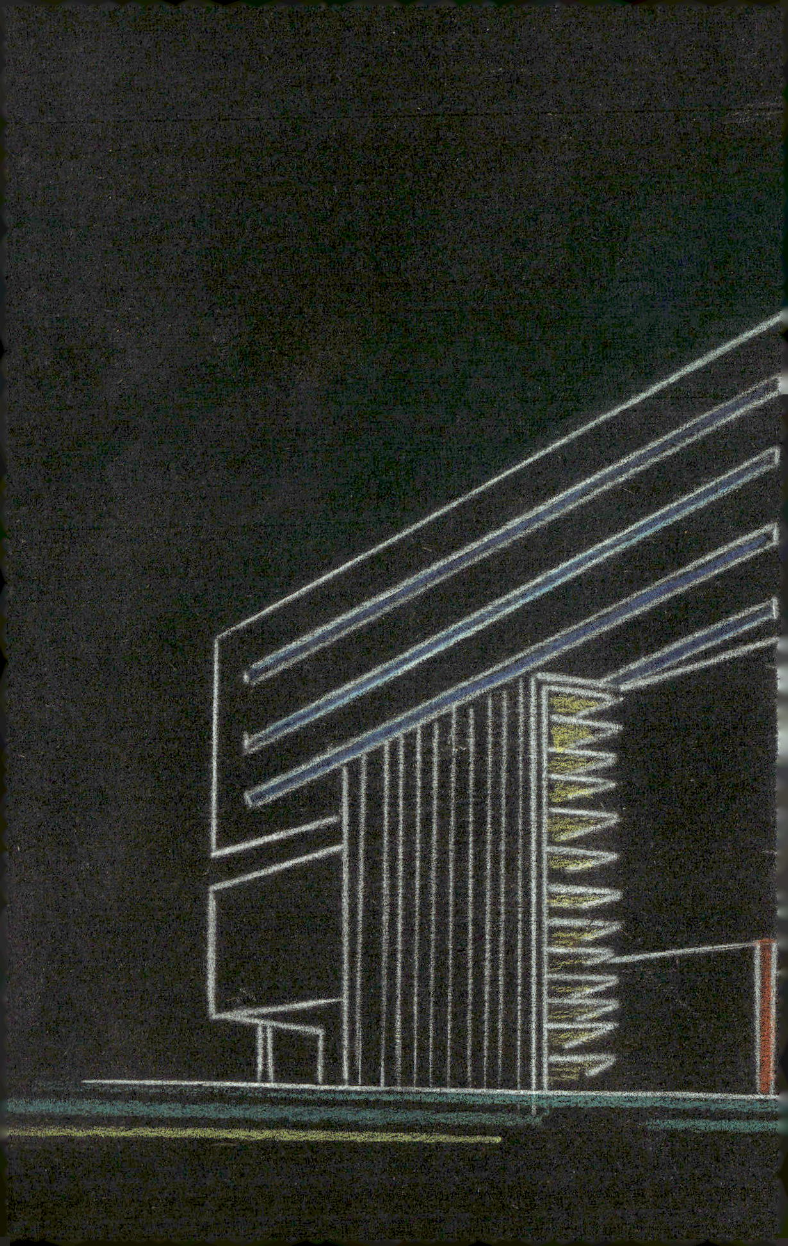

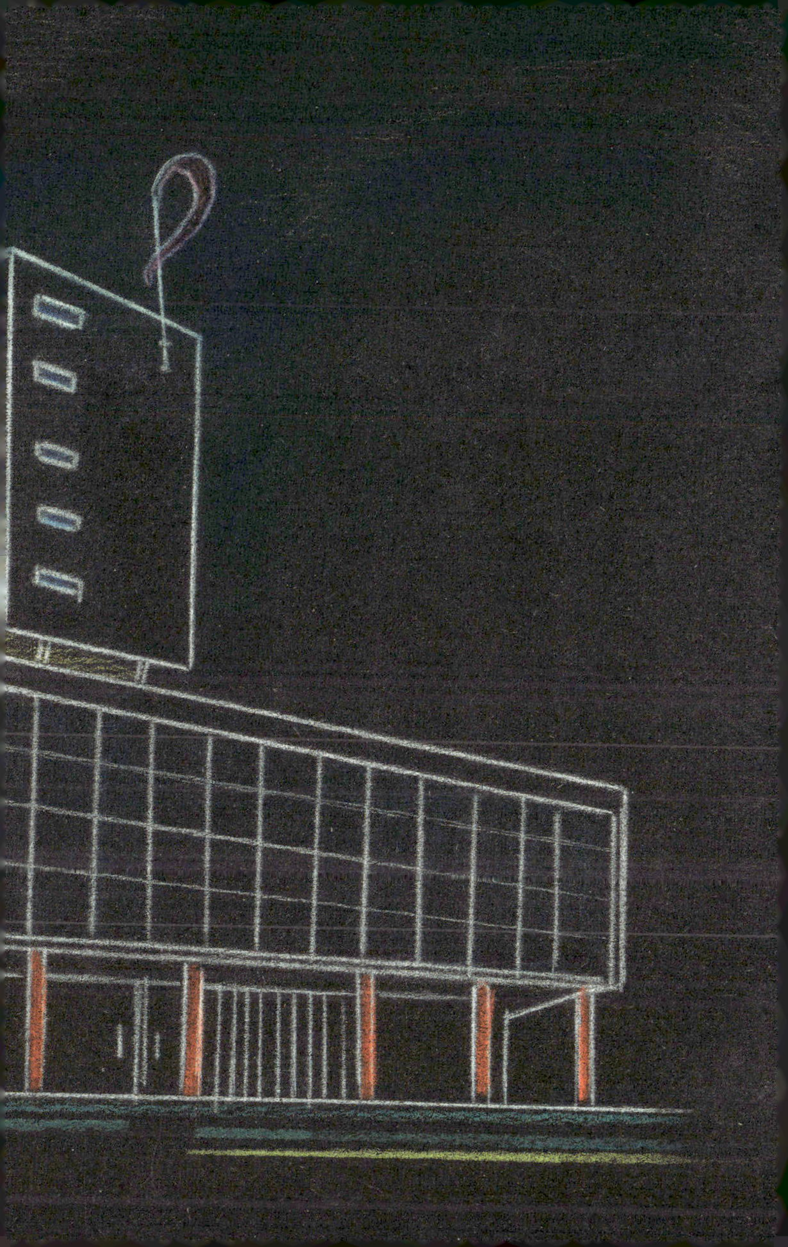

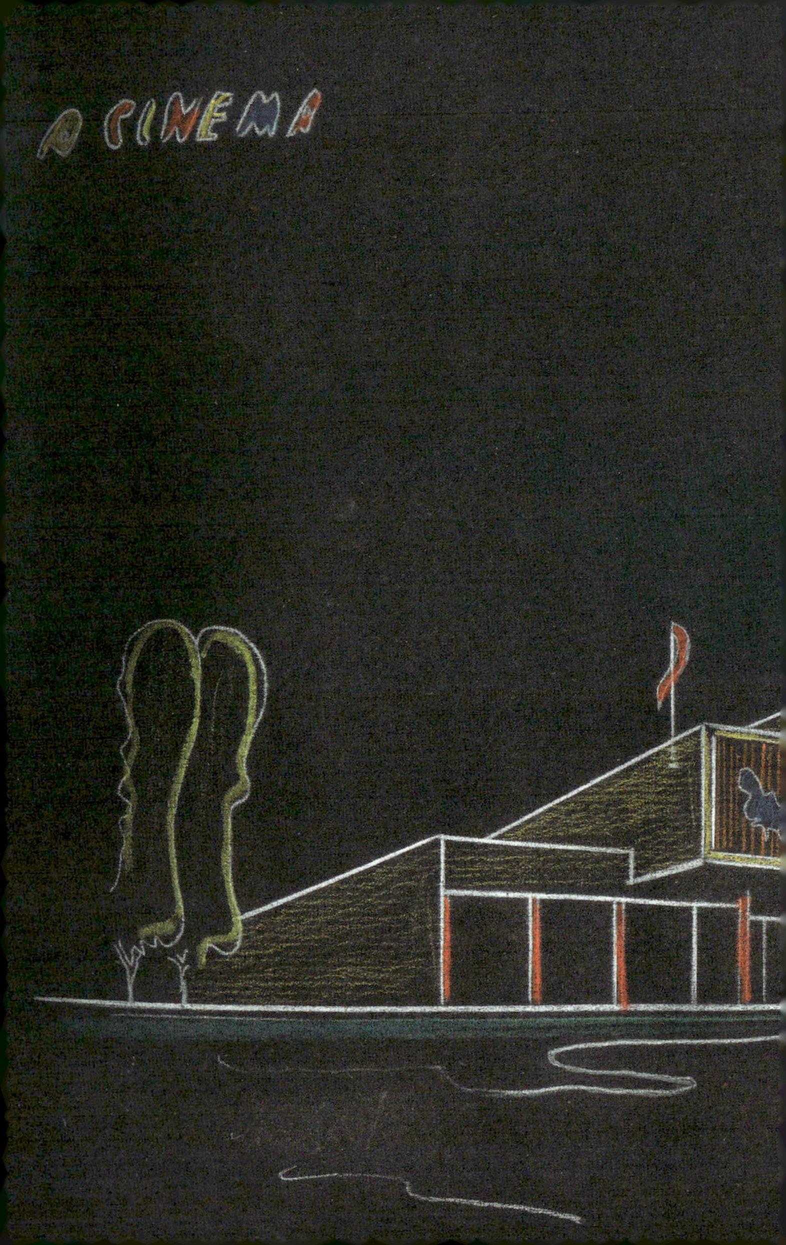
A CINEMA

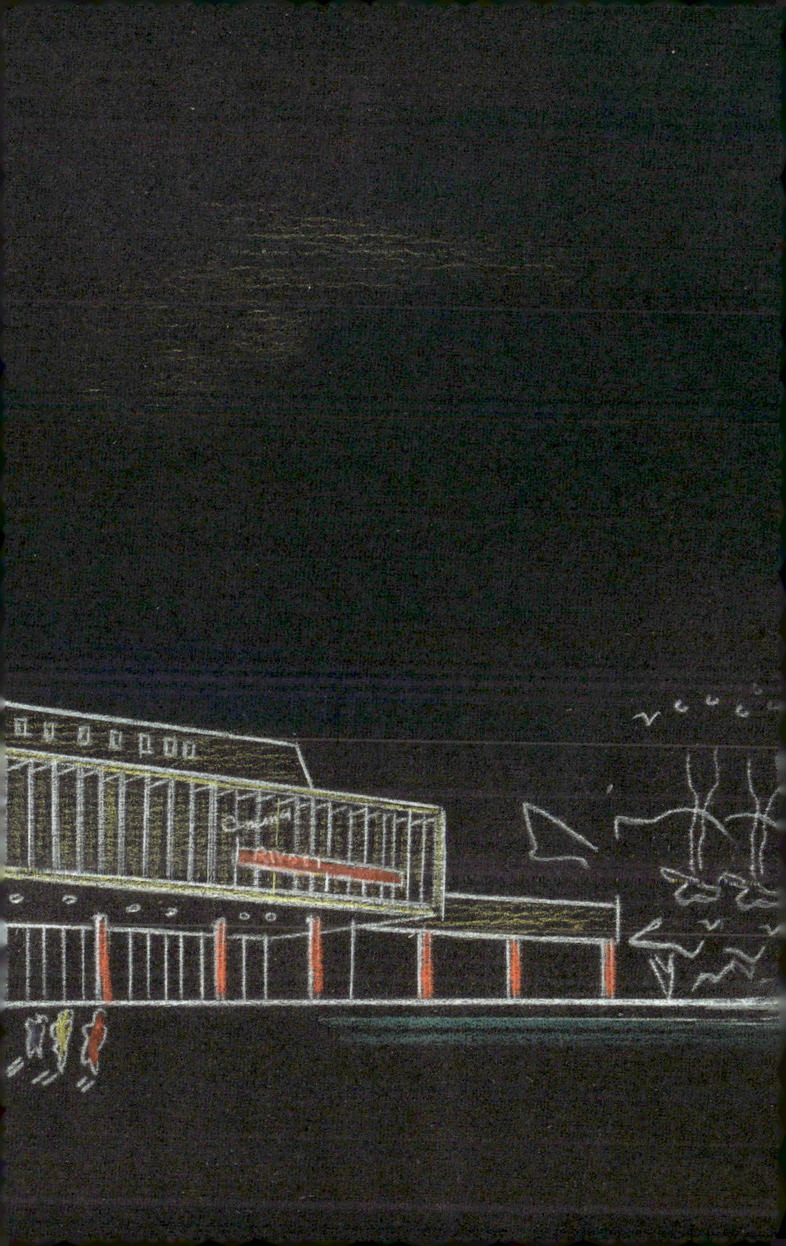

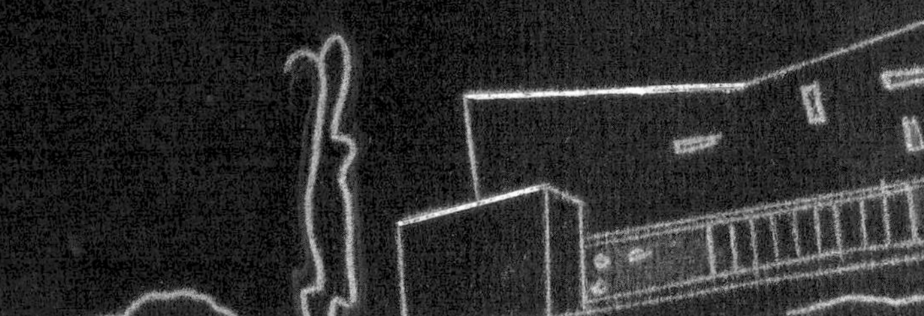

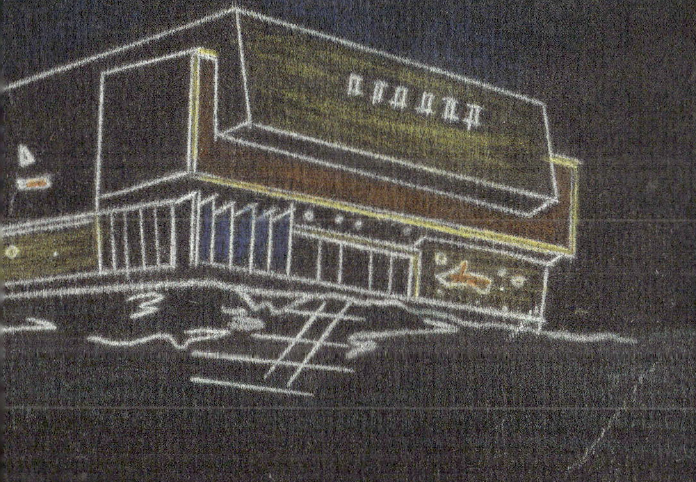

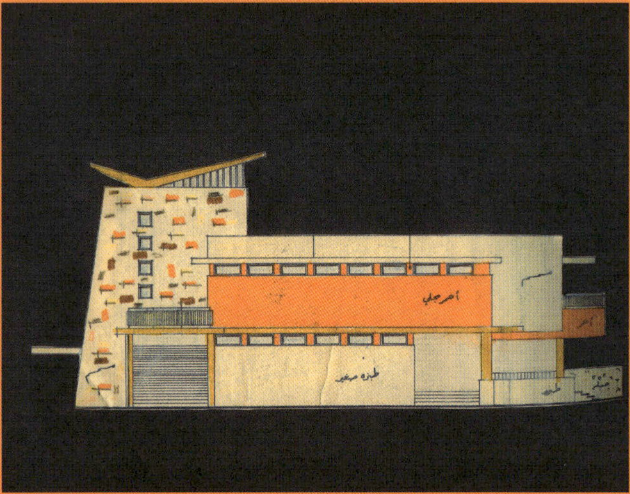

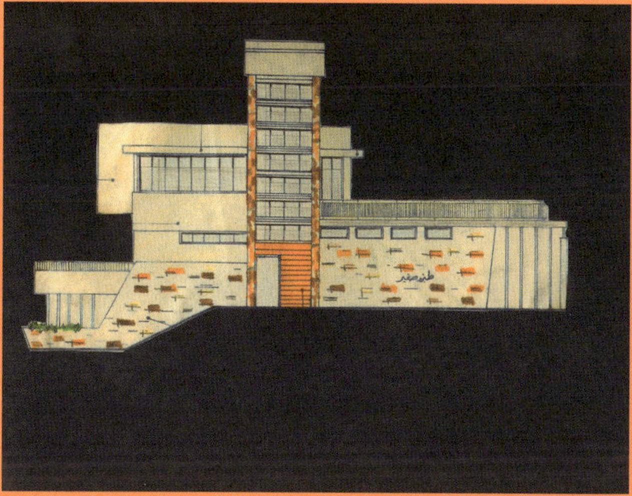

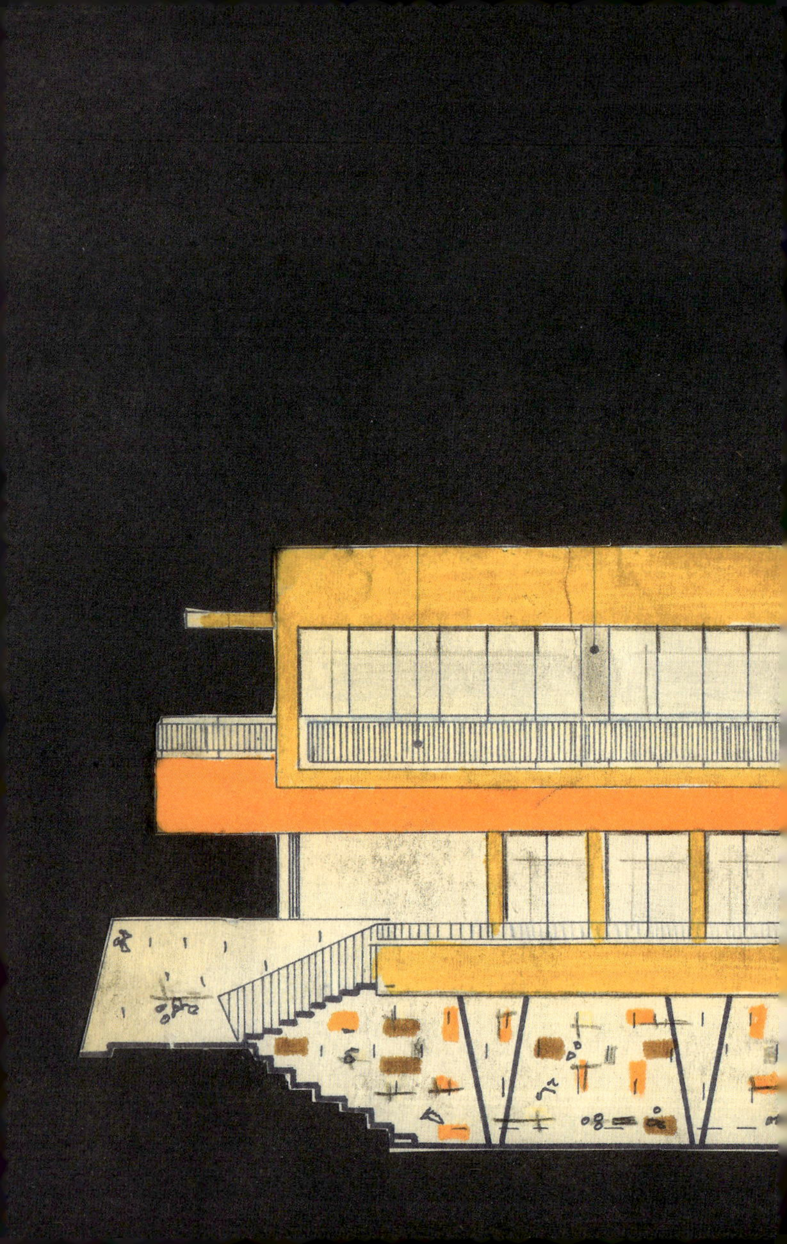

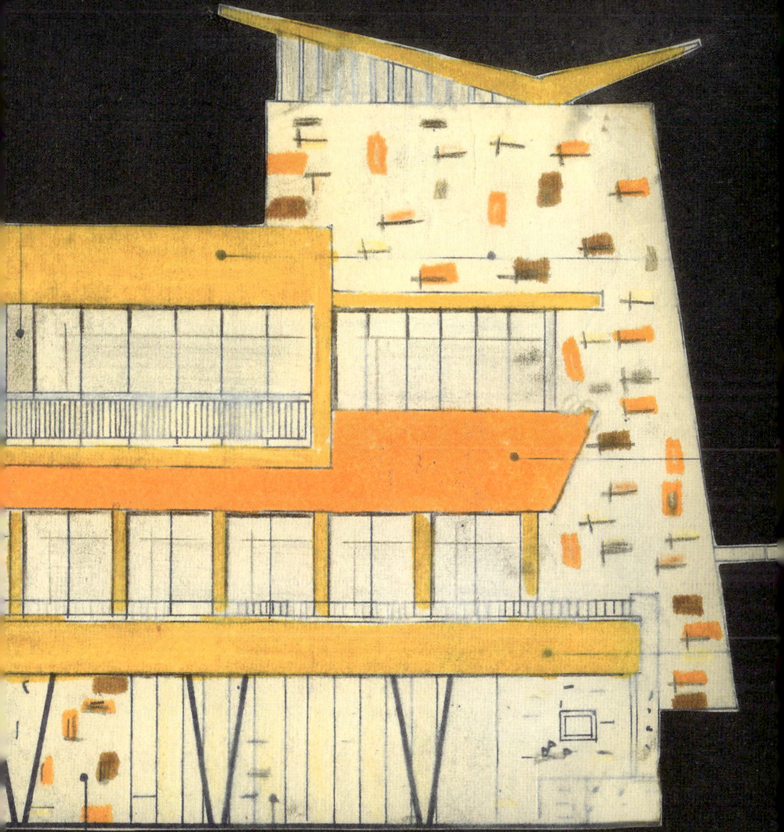

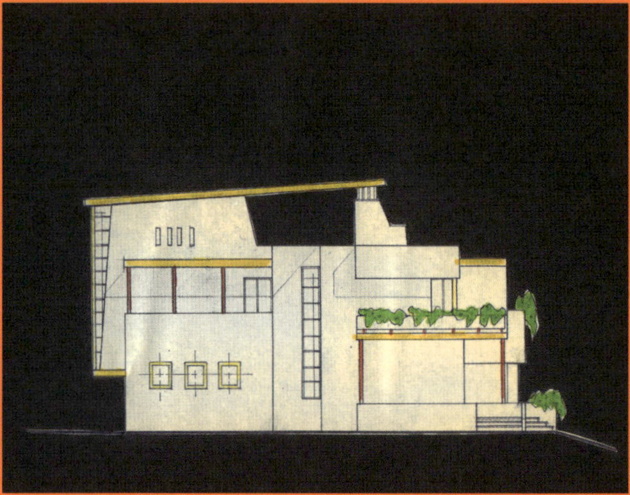

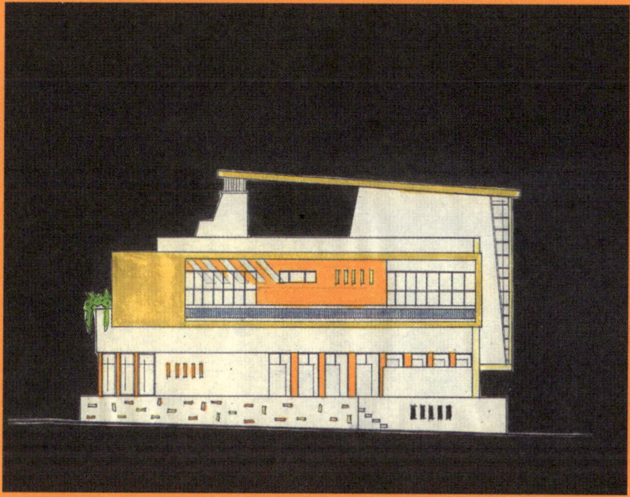

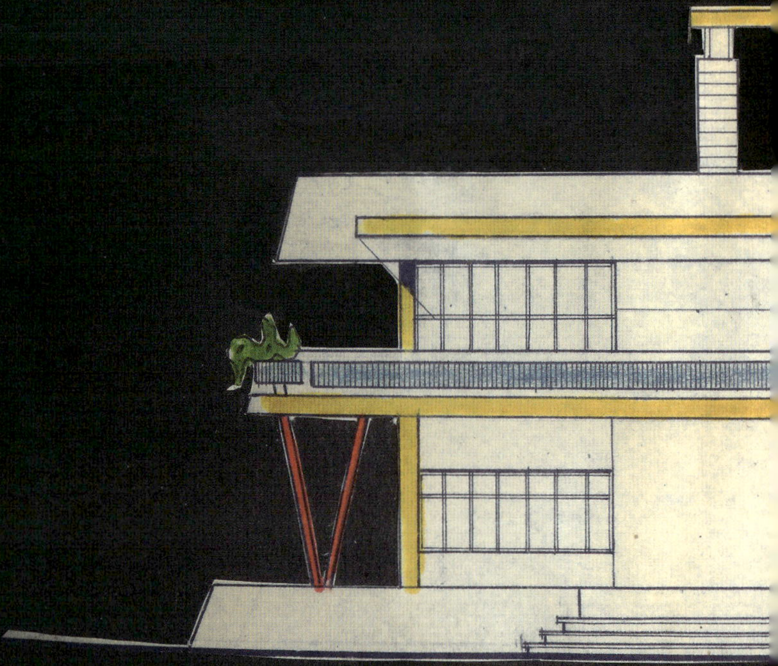

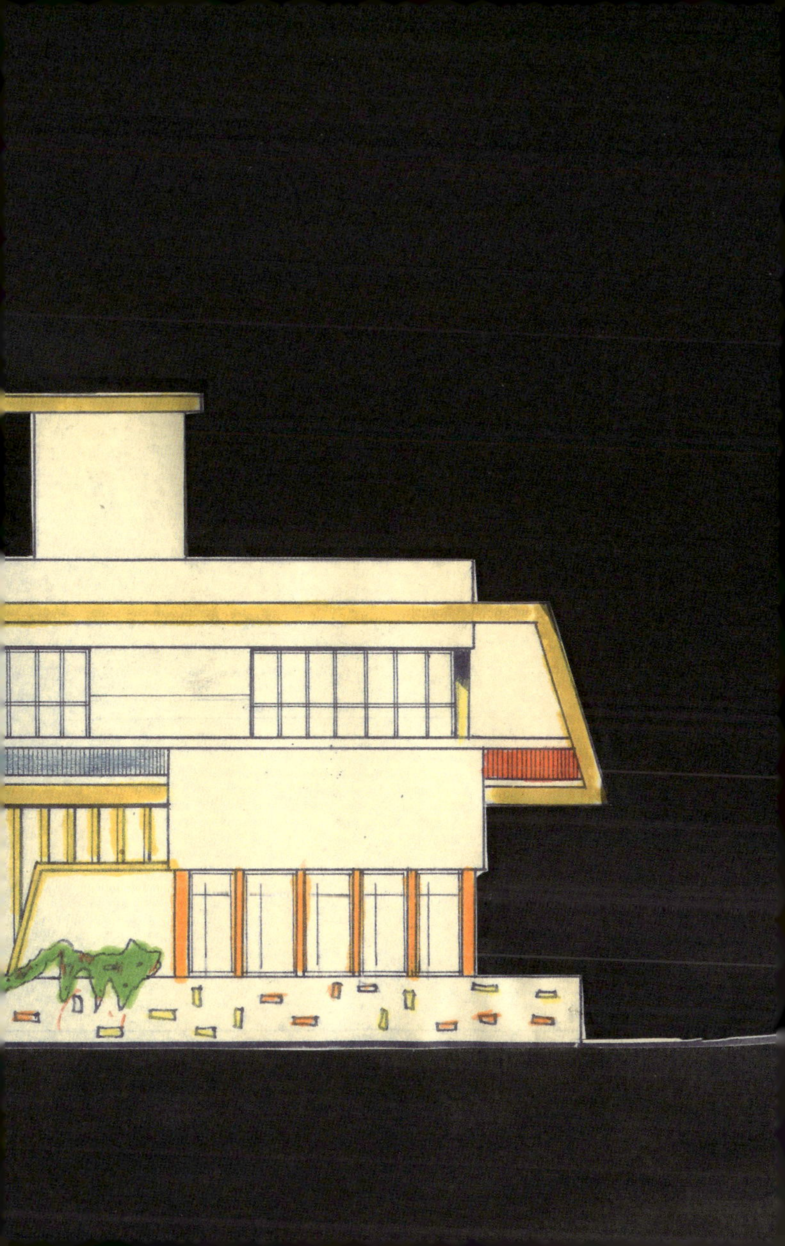

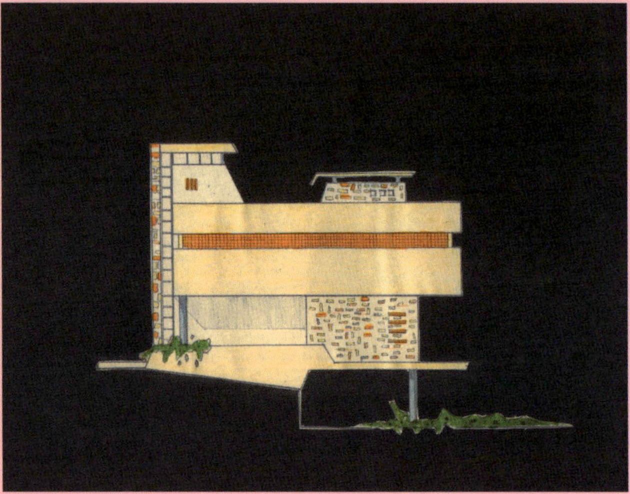

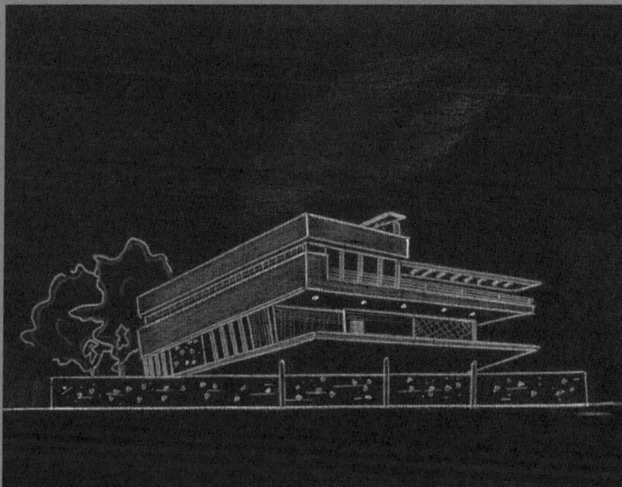

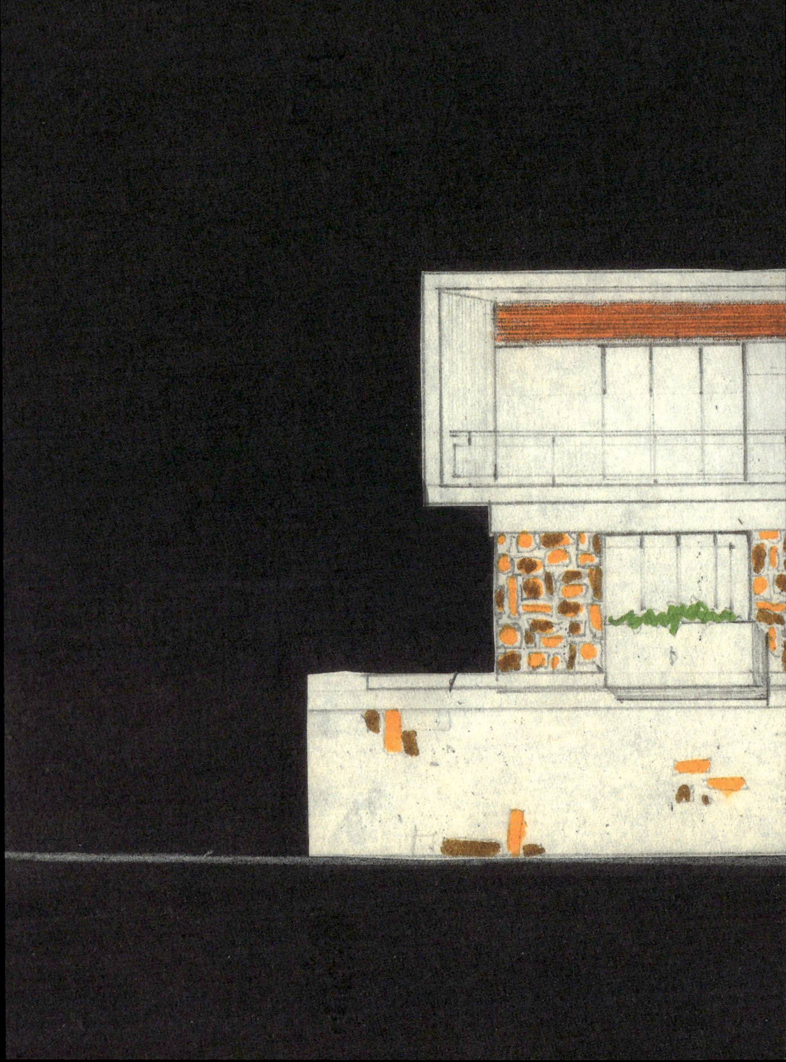

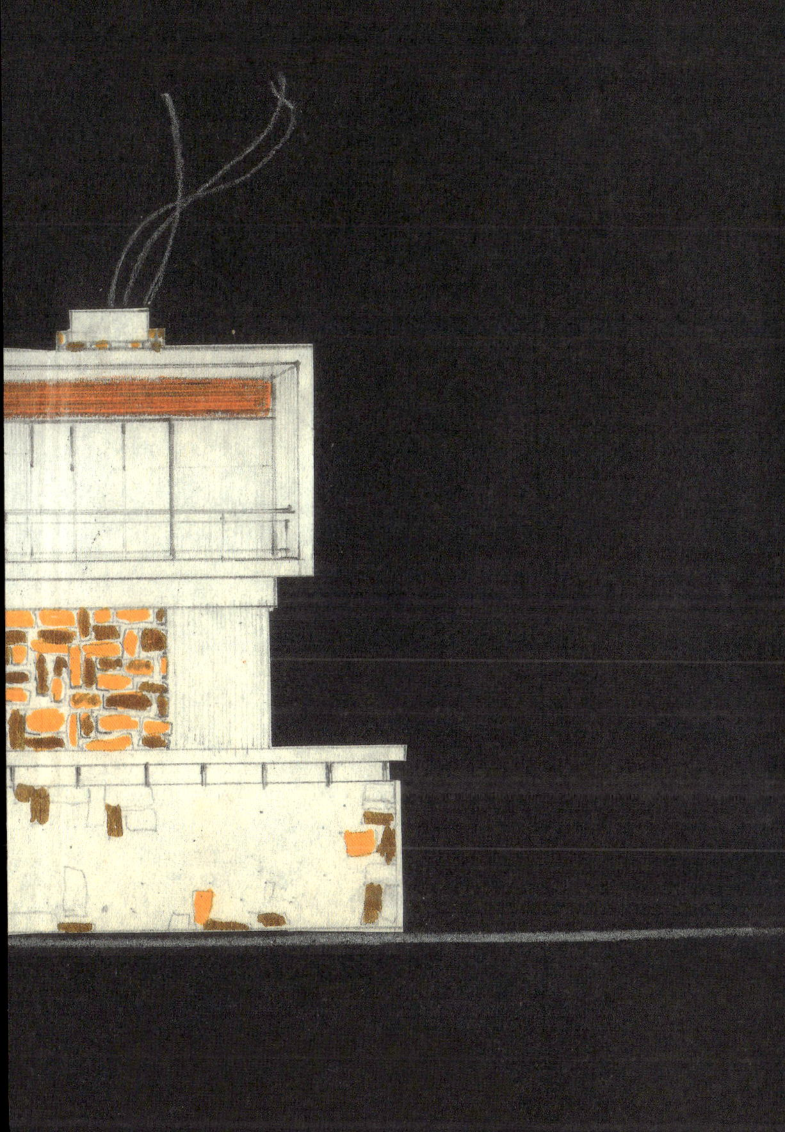

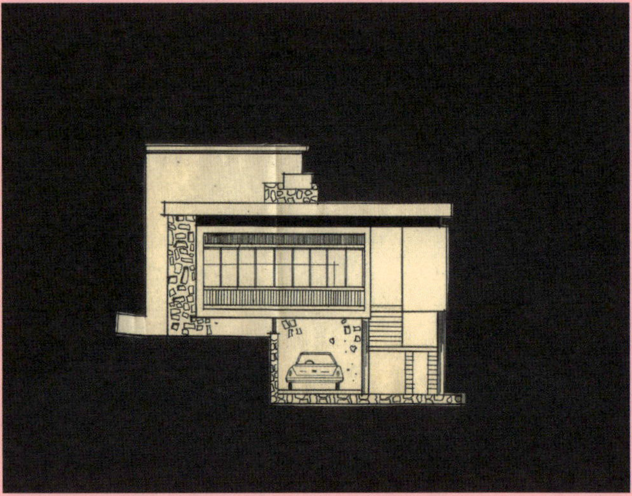

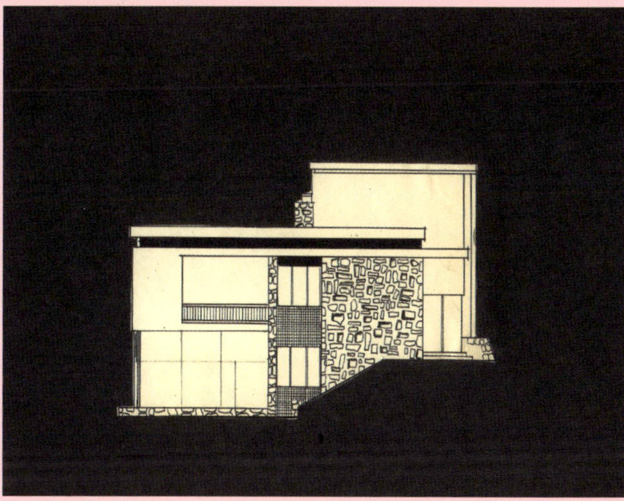

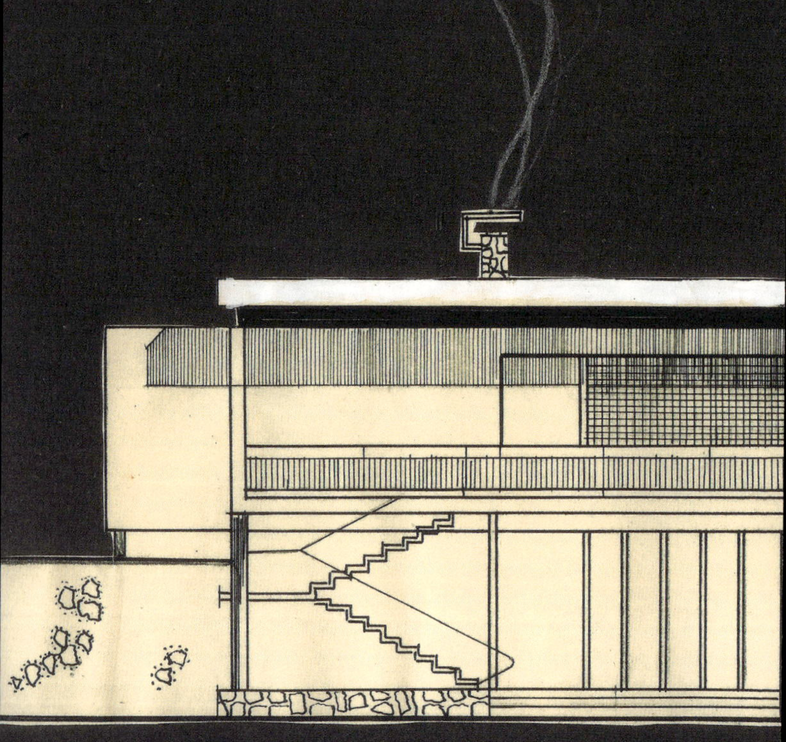

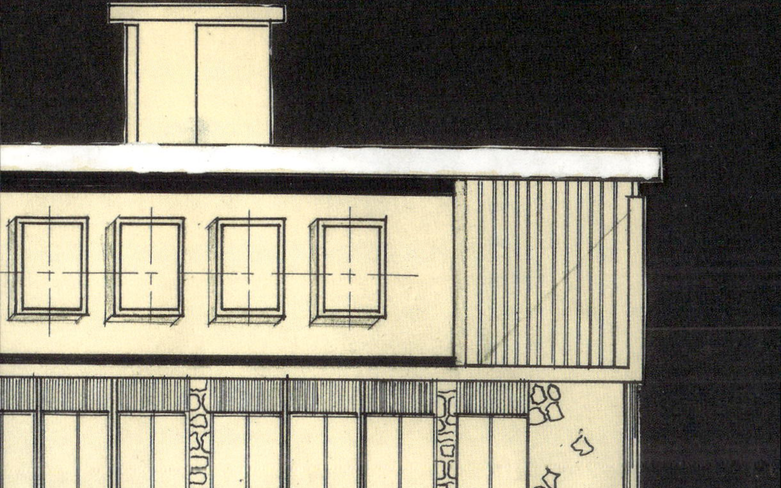

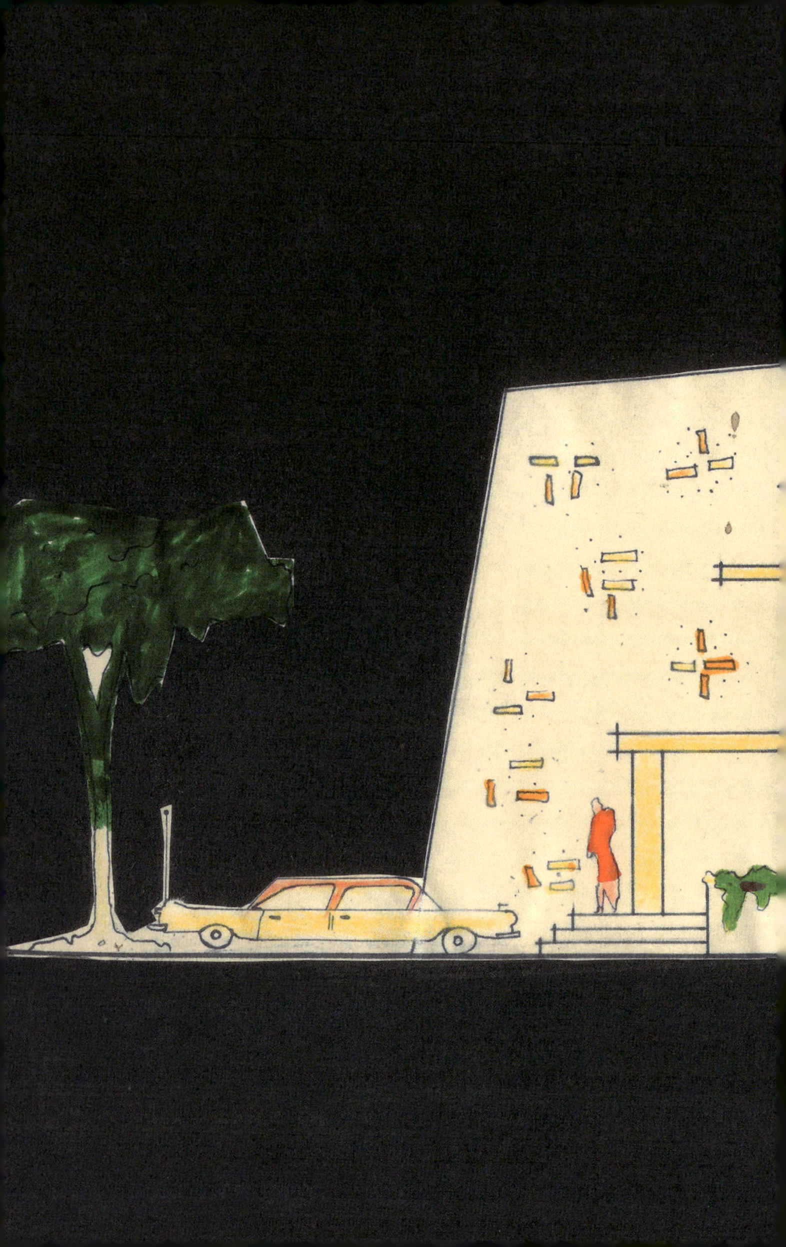

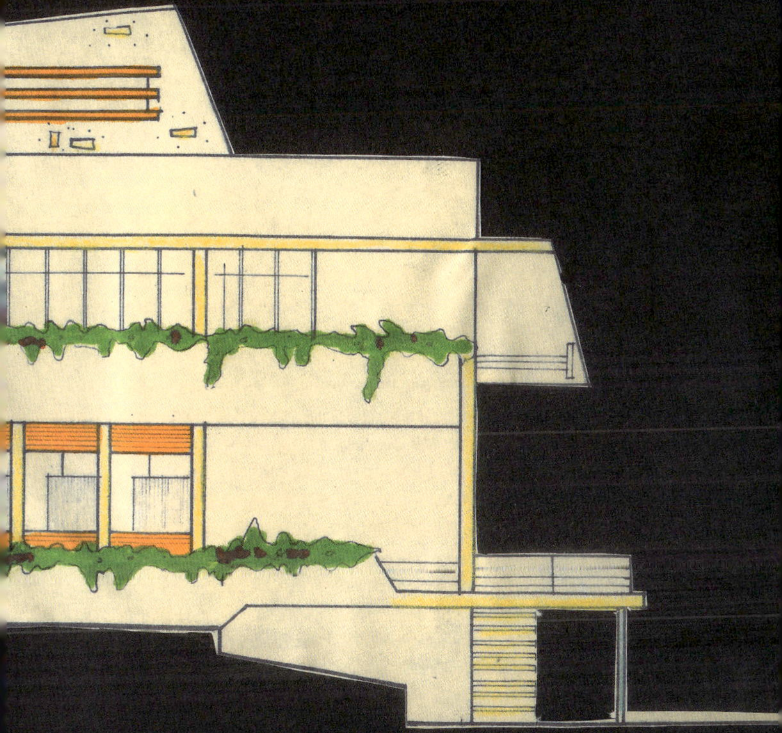

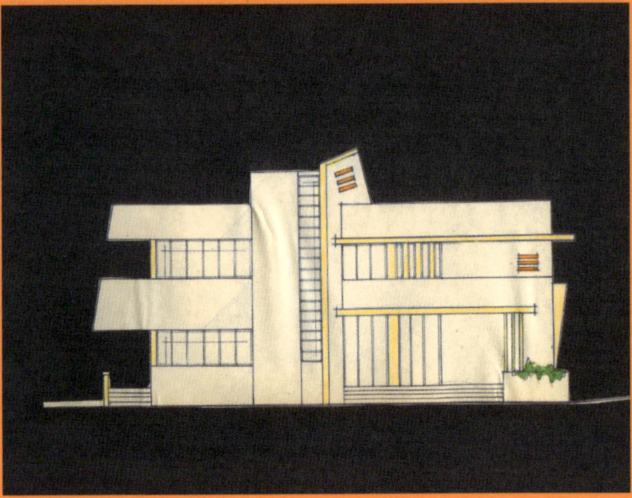

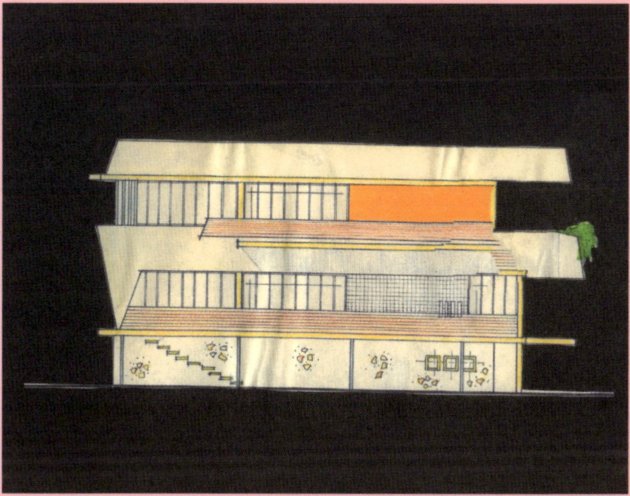

A CASINO

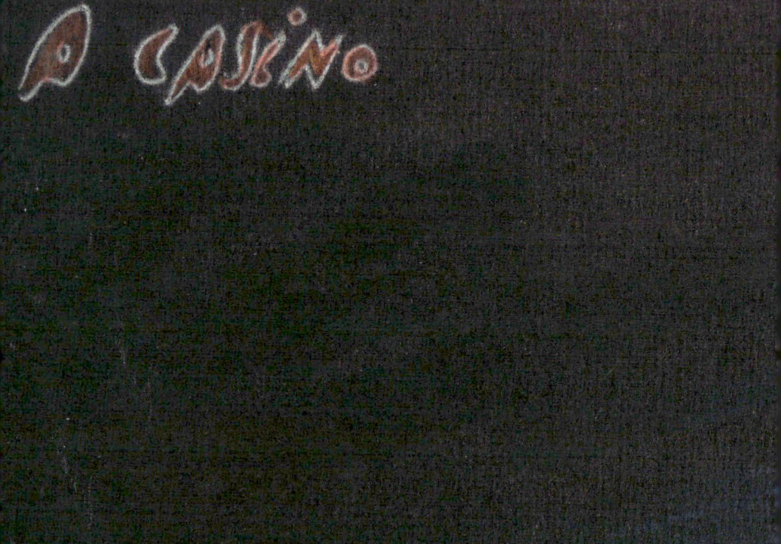

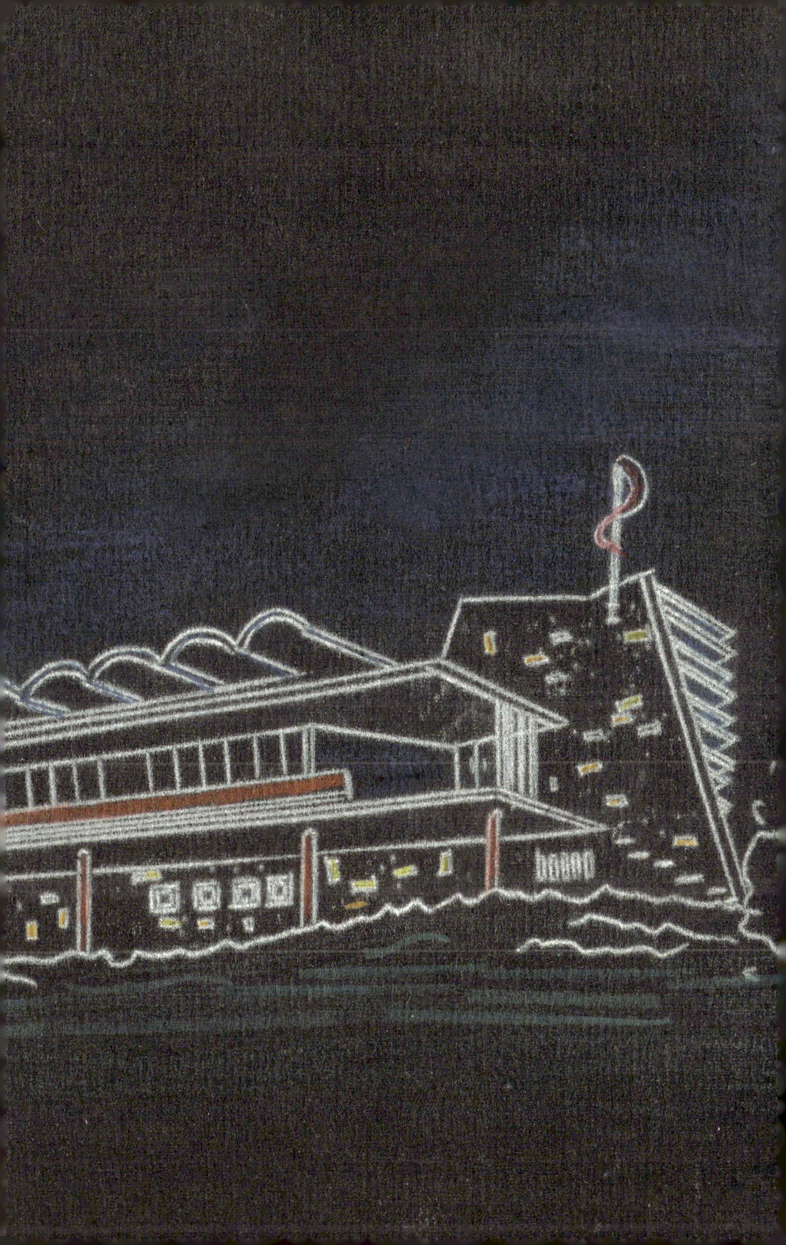

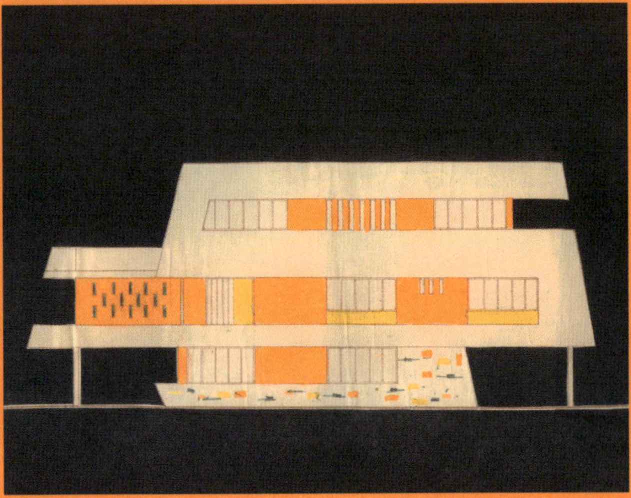

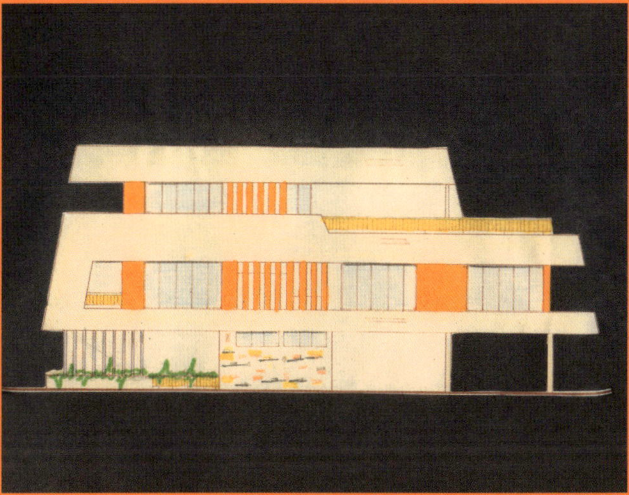

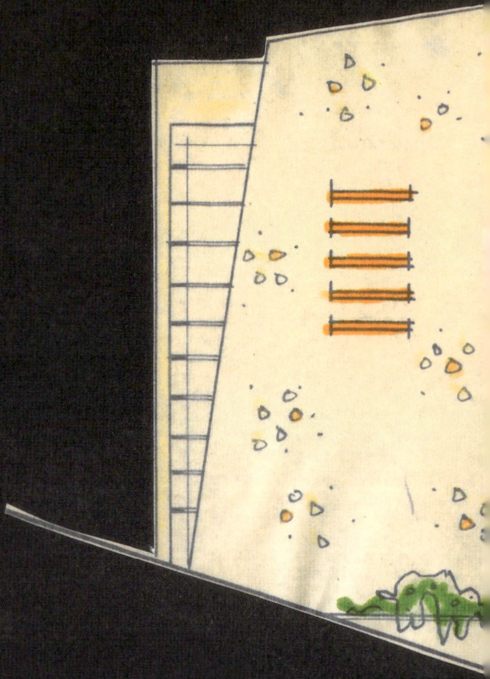

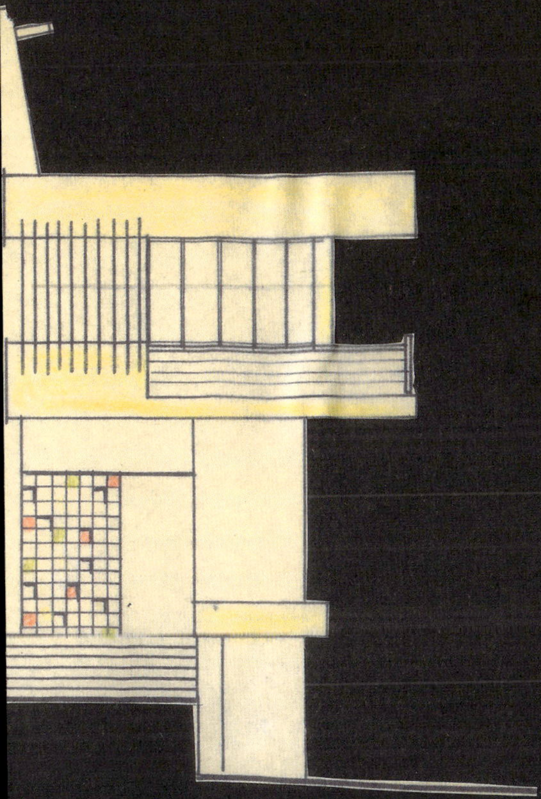

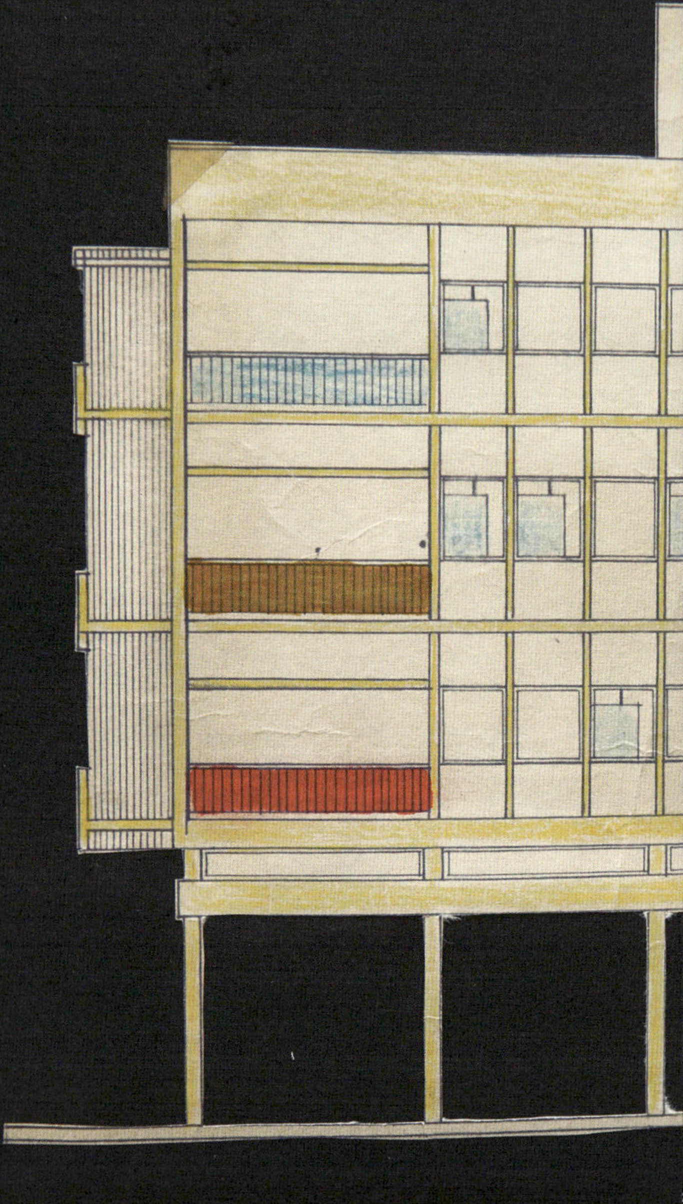

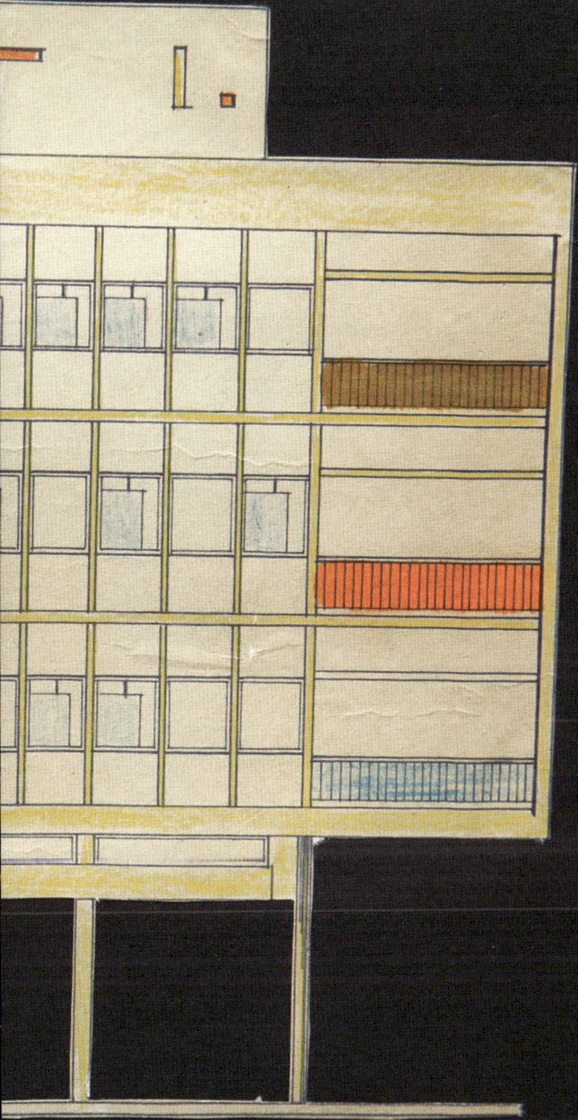

جامعاتنا. لا نريد فعلاً لفت أي انتباه إضافي». شكرته على وقته وخرجت. في الخارج، استخرجت هاتفي النقال من حقيبتي، وتوجهت إلى المبنى والتقطت صورة. لاحظت تمثالاً على عمود قرب الأعمدة الخرسانية القصيرة التي تحمل قسماً من المبنى الذي صممه هاني عرفات. اقتربت منه ووجدت أنه تمثال لواحد من مؤسسي الجامعة: عالم الرياضيات والمُنظِّر والناشط قدري طوقان. تتكشف أعمال هاني عرفات بتدرج بطيء. تظهر شيئاً، ثم تصبح شيئاً آخر. تبدو كأنها ذات طوايا، خام، وملونة بأنواع الحجر (مسمسم أو طبزة أو أحمر مجلي). ثم تتغير مرة أخرى عندما تواجه كتلا مكعبة على جهة المبنى الأخرى.

درس عرفات العمارة في جامعة القاهرة وتخرج عام ١٩٥٥، وبدأ عمله في الكويت ثم انتقل إلى هيئة الأشغال العامة في عمّان إلى جانب عمله الخاص، قبل أن يصبح المعماري الرئيس في بلدية نابلس. مع عدد من المعماريين في وقته، كان عرفات بدون شك جزءاً من حركة استقلال مدني ونُفي كذلك لبعض الوقت. أرتني ابنته ريما عرفات، وهي معمارية نشطة بشكل رائع وتعيش في نابلس، الرسومات التالية للمباني المنفذة وغير المنفذة من أعماله.

يا عزيزتي» أجابت، «سوف أوصلك به». «مرحبا، اسمي عريب طوقان. أنا مديرة برنامج دراسة الإعلام في جامعة القدس. أريد فقط أن التقط صورة واحدة للمبنى الرئيسي لجامعة النجاح»، شرحت مرة أخرى. «أنت تتحدثين من البوابة، صحيح؟» سألني نائب الرئيس. أجبت بنعم، فقال «رجاءً تعالي لشرب الشاي وعرفي عن نفسك. أحتاج إلى استخراج تصريح. أخبرتني مساعدتي بأنهم حولوك عدة مرات. أعتذر بشدة أن الأمر تعقد لهذه الدرجة! » صعدت إلى مكتبه، وتحدثت إليه، ووجدته مثيراً للاهتمام. كذلك تحدثنا عن انسحاب جامعة برانديس من دعم جامعة القدس لأن الأولى ارتعبت من صور نشرت على تويتر لتجمع طلابي لحركة الجهاد الإسلامي الفلسطيني حدث في حرم الجامعة. اتصل بمرؤوسه، شرح طلبي، استمع إلى جواب طويل، ثم وضع السماعة. «أنا آسف جداً، لا يمكنك أن تلتقطي الصورة في النهاية.» سألت لماذا، (وأشعر بأن نبرة صوتي حملت شيئاً من الوقاحة التي ما زلت نادمة عليها إلى الآن). قال لي «جزء من المبنى الذي أنت مهتمة به هو الآن قسم علوم الشريعة. يحب الإسرائيليون أي سبب لاقتحام

أريد أن ألتقط صورة جيدة وبكاميرا فاخرة لواحدة من مباني هاني عرفات. أحضرت واحدة معي أثناء زيارتي لنابلس حتى أتمكن من تصوير مبنى من تصميمه في حرم جامعة النجاح الوطنية. استوقفني الأمن عندما عبرت من البوابة. أخبرتهم بأني أود أن ألتقط صورة المبنى الرئيسي للجامعة. استدار الحارسان ونظرا إلى المبنى ثم قال أحدهما: «تفضلي». «لشو هالصورة؟» سأل الآخر. «بحبه»، أجبت. «حسناً، عليكِ أن تحصلي على إذن من مكتب العلاقات العامة قبل أن تدخلي.» توجه الحارس الأول، وكان أكثر تراخياً، نحو الهاتف واتصل بالمكتب شارحاً لهم الموقف. قضى وقتا وهو يستمع ويهز برأسه قبل أن يضع السماعة ويعود إلي، «آسف»، قال، «تسرعت في الكلام. عليكِ أن تتصلي بنائب الرئيس شخصياً وتشرحي له.» التقط السماعة وطلب الرقم الفرعي، ثم تناولت السماعة الدافئة من يده، «ألو؟» «مرحبا، اسمي عريب طوقان. أنا فنانة ومهتمة بشغل المعماري هاني عرفات، إللي عمل المبنى في جامعتكم في بداية الستينات. بحب إني آخد له صورة فوتوغرافية.»

«عليكِ أن تتحدثي إلى نائب الرئيس عن هذا الأمر

هاني عرفات،
لون الشمس

Fouad Sayegh,
In Spite of All

Fouad Sayegh tells me that his office was burned down during the events of Black September in Jordan. Original photographs, plans, and drawings of his earlier works no longer exist. There are some low-resolution photographs that his daughter, also an architect, digitally archived for him. He only seemed to recall designing four buildings in Palestine, all before 1967; one of them is the post office on Salah ad-Din Street in Jerusalem. A floor of that building was recently bought by the property developers Ateret Cohanim to house a Jewish Orthodox religious school, part of their mission to create a Jewish majority in East Jerusalem. He was not aware of this.

The second was the Hilton Carlton between Ramallah and Jerusalem. It was built for Mohammad Jowdat Ghosheh, originally as a two-facing hospital. It was conceived in 1959, and it opened in 1963.

Sayegh was a fresh graduate from Cairo at the time, and seemingly wanted to be as ahistorical as possible in his final design: clean geometric lines, starkly cut reinforced concrete with a mild pink stone facade on the side. When a Hilton hotel opened in Tel Aviv, Israeli soldiers confiscated Ghosheh's "Hilton" sign. By the early 1970s, the Israeli military were using it as a base. Eventually, Al-Quds University transformed it into a women's dormitory for their nursing school, until a community-led television station was born there in 1996—where *Shara'a Sim Sim*, an Arabic spin-off of *Sesame Street* was produced. Most recently, Israeli soldiers confiscated the radio transmitter and shut down the community channel. They now air as *Hona Al Quds* on YouTube and other platforms.

نموذج رقم "٤"

المملكه الاردنيه الهاشميــــــــــه
وزارة الاقتصاد الوطــــــني
قانون تسجيل الاسماء التجاريه رقم ٣٠ لسنـــــة١٩٥٣
الذيل الثالـــــث
((للقرار الصادر بمقتضى هذا القانــــــون))

==========

حضرة : السيد محمد جودت غوشــــه

من : رام الله ـ الشرفه ـ البيره

الذى يتعاطى : اوتيل

اشهد ان الاسم التجارى : فندق هيلتون

قد سجل في السجل وادخل في فهرس التسجيل تحت رقم(٢١٣٣)
بمقتضى ومع مراعاة احكام قانون تسجيل الاسماء التجاريه لسنة ٩٥٣ والقرار الصادر
بمقتضاه كاسمك /كاسمكم التجارى

صدرت بتوقيعي في هذا اليوم الثالث والعشرون شهر حزيران سنة ١٩٦٣

مسجل الاسماء التجاريــــــه

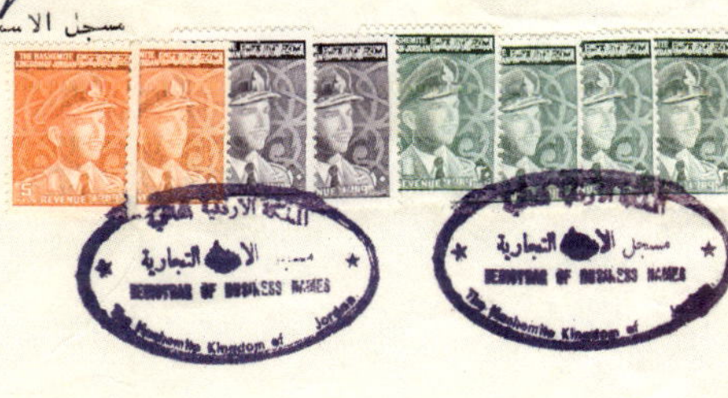

Page 165:
Commercial registration of Hilton Hotel Jerusalem-Bireh at the Ministry of National Economy, Jordan, 1963

Pages 167–88:
A 2014 film script produced by Casey Asprooth-Jackson, in collaboration with Fadi Abu Nemeh and Salah Shbak, on the building—now Al-Quds University's Institute for Modern Media

ARLTON HOTEL

RAMALLAH — JERUSALEM

Tel. 293 RAMALLAH
352 JERUSALEM

P. O. B. RAMALLAH

P. O. B. 35 JERUSALEM

فندق كارلتون

رام الله – القدس

تلفون ٢٩٣ رام الله
٣٥٢ القدس

صندوق البريد رام الله
صندوق البريد ٣٥ القدس

EXCERPT FROM A BUILDING IN PROGRESS

Written by

CAJ

12 Nablus Rd, Jerusalem/Bireh/Ramallah
054/056/0599309106

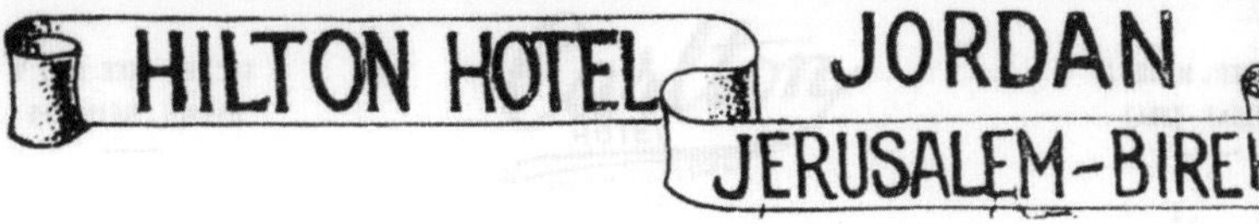

INT. LAPTOP MONITOR - 12:02 PM

"Skype" is open and we hear the chirp of a call's beginning. CALLER is clicking away on his laptop and his voice is heard clearly throughout the conversation to come. As he waits for his rings to be answered, he hums a four-note tune. The second voice, coming through the computer's speakers, is distorted but audible. *Ring ring ri-*

AUTOMATED RESPONSE 1 (O.S.)
Hilton...

CALLER (O.S.)
Hello?

AUTOMATED RESPONSE 1 (O.S.)
(hurried)
Sorry, this inbox is full. You cannot leave a message for this user. You may now hang-up or enter another extension.

CALLER (O.S.)
Damn...

The cursor hovers over the red phone icon, a click is heard, and the call ends. More clicking, humming. Another chirp and the rings return.

AUTOMATED RESPONSE 2 (O.S.)
Hilton Worldwide -

AUTOMATED RESPONSE 3 (O.S.)
- is not available. Record your message after the tone. When you're finished you can hang up or press one for more options.

Beep

CALLER (O.S.)
Uh, hi there. Um, I'm looking for some information regarding a hotel of your brand that may or may not have existed in Jerusalem in the 1960s. If you would please, uh, return this call via email, uh, I would really appreciate...

CALLER's voice trails off and the call ends. He hums faster now.

CUT TO:

. O. B. 337 - TEL. 392
RAMALLAH - JORDAN

Carlton
HOTEL
PROP M. J. GHOSHEH

EL - BIREH - JERUSALEM
CABLE : CARLTAC

Ref. :

Date

INT. UNIVERSITY CLASSROOM - 4:30 PM

A small class is gathered around a table covered in documents. The topic of discussion is the building they are sitting in, and the disputed history surrounding it. PROFESSOR 1 leads the conversation among the four STUDENTS while PROFESSOR 2 sits at a laptop preparing an image to share with the group. A VISITOR observes the conversation, taking notes.

AERIAL VIEW OF TABLE

STUDENT 1
I spoke with a woman who worked here when it was a nursing college. She didn't know much about the hotel, but she had loads of stories about the school. Apparently the outside of the building used to be painted blue.

PROFESSOR 1
Huh. It would be great to have a picture from that time. What did you think of the photos Ghosheh gave us?

CLOSE-UP ON NOTEBOOK

The VISITOR is scribbling a sentence as the class continues their discussion. His notes at the top of the page read:

"Ghosheh loan 4 hospital '61. Bank nixes hospital, wants hotel > Carlton Opens w/ Ghosheh wedding 1962. Hilton by '63 (why? actually registered Carlton/Hilton?) IOF occupies building '67, steals Hilton sign, military outpost (on high hill) until '70. Ownership changes, Armenian priest and settler org (!) have stake > PLO steps in by late 70s takes ownership of building"

STUDENT 2 (O.S.)
The hotel documents are interesting but the photos are plain. As I was scanning them I was hoping to find something with a new story, but it comes off as a normal hotel.

PROFESSOR 1
There were more photos at the house than there are here. Ghosheh censored what he let us borrow.
(MORE)

PROFESSOR 1 (CONT'D)
I'll try and convince him to give us the rest, but I don't know. If not, the work becomes about censorship, missing information, constructed memory.

The VISITOR finishes his sentence. It reads:

"nursing hospital, blue building? Ghosheh censorship, recover remaining photos."

FADE TO:

INT. LAPTOP MONITOR - 12:10

CALLER is humming as the Skype call rings. A phone number with a Jordanian country code blinks in the center of the program window.

DOUBLE TREE REP 1
Thank you for calling Double Tree Aqaba, Omar speaking, how my I help you?

CALLER
Hi there, Omar. I'm a researcher looking into the history of a Hilton hotel that was built in the region in the, um, early 60s, and I was hoping you could point me toward a PR rep or perhaps someone who has -

DOUBLE TREE REP 1
(interrupting)
One moment, uh, I will transfer you to my PR, uh, relation.

CALLER
Thank you very much.

AUTOMATED RESPONSE 4
Welcome! To Double Tree by Hilton, Aqaba. Here our gen- Welcome! To Double Tree by Hilton, Aqaba. Here our generous hospitality starts with a chocolate chip cookie to give you the feeling of true care and comfort.
(MORE)

AUTOMATED RESPONSE 4 (CONT'D)

You can further spoil yourself at our spacious, superior and deluxe guest rooms, furnished with all amenities to enjoy an exclusive stay. The Italian style hotel offers fully equipped guest rooms and suites for your convenience. Indulge in our assorted restaurants and bars. King's Grill is serving the finest steak and wine from 6:30 to 11 PM. D-Lounge, offering tempting delicacies from 10 PM to 3 AM. Gusto, the all day dining restaurant with international specialty and the infinity pool bar, featuring scenic views, light snacks and refreshing drinks from 10 AM to 10 PM. We would be pleased to have you and make your stay unforgettable. For more information or reservations, please contact us on 96232093209. Or the email address: doubletreeaqaba.info @hilton.com...Welcome! To Double Tree by Hilton, Aqaba. Here our gen- Welcome! To Double Tree by Hilton, Aqaba. Here our generous hospitality starts with a chocolate chip cookie to give you the feeling of true care and comfort. You can further spoil yourself at our spacious, superior and deluxe guest rooms, furnished with all amenities to enjoy an exclusive stay. The Italian style hotel offers fully equipped guest rooms and suites for your convenience. Indulge in our assorted restaurants and bars. King's Grill is serving the finest steak and wine from 6:30 to 11 PM. D-Lounge, offering tempting delicacies from 10 PM to 3 AM. Gusto, the all day dining restaurant with international specialty and the infinity pool bar, featuring scenic views, light snacks and refreshing drinks from 10 AM to 10 PM. We would be pleased to have you and make your stay unforgettable. For more information or reservations, please contact us on 96232093209. Or the email address: doubletreeaqaba.info @hilton.com...Welcome!

(MORE)

HILTON HOTEL JORDAN JERUSALEM-BIRE

AUTOMATED RESPONSE 4 (CONT'D)

To Double Tree by Hilton, Aqaba. Here our gen- Welcome! To Double Tree by Hilton, Aqaba. Here our generous hospitality starts with a chocolate chip cookie to give you the feeling of true care and comfort. You can further spoil yourself at our spacious, superior and deluxe guest rooms, furnished with all amenities to enjoy an exclusive stay. The Italian style hotel offers fully equipped guest rooms and suites for your convenience. Indulge in our assorted restaurants and bars. King's Grill is serving the finest steak and wine from 6:30 to 11 PM. D-Lounge, offering tempting delicacies from 10 PM to 3 AM. Gusto, the all day dining restaurant with international specialty and the infinity pool bar, featuring scenic views, light snacks and refreshing drinks from 10 AM to 10 PM. We would be pleased to have you and make your stay unforgettable. For more information or reservations, please contact us on 96232093209. Or the email address: doubletreeaqaba.info @hilton.com...Welcome! To Double Tree by Hilton -

A click is heard and the call ends abruptly.

CUT TO:

INT. UNIVERSITY CLASSROOM - 4:45 PM

A class has just finished viewing a projection of videos prepared for their collaborative show. The program window is open on the laptop computer from which the projection finds its source. The top of the window reads "VLC media player"; just below it, "IMM.newcut"; and below that, "Tryptic 1." The STUDENTS and PROFESSORS critique the work, discussing plans for revision. Once again, a VISITOR takes notes as the conversation progresses.

CLOSE-UP ON PROJECTION SCREEN

PROFESSOR 2 (O.S.)
I think there are a lot of strong images here, ya know, I really do. The building is front and center, and we're getting a good sense of the history. I just think it would all benefit from more work on the audio.

STUDENT 2 (O.S.)
I was wondering what these might feel like with more sound.

PROFESSOR 2 (O.S.)
Not just more sound, but well-recorded audio to work with the video. Silence has its place, but I think finding an interesting way to break that silence can be a more effective strategy.

STUDENT 3 (O.S.)
At least for my video I didn't want to add too much more sound than I have here. I tried adding a track from a crowded cafeteria and it didn't work, so I decided to leave it clean.

CLOSE-UP ON NOTEBOOK

The VISITOR is scribbling a sentence as the class continues their discussion. His notes at the top of the page read:

"SALAH: solid cuts, re-shoot hallway shot in reverse on towel. everyone does elevator; it's tired. memo against weird sound at start - definitely keep. Me: out of sync is crucial, multiple monitors. materiality still key: big vinyl, vollume paper script, digi material in source 1."

PROFESSOR 2 (O.S.)
Ya I think the school-noise thing is overdone. I was speaking more about the second video.

PROFESSOR 1 (O.S.)
I totally disagree. The silence and the duration are what make this piece work.
(MORE)

HILTON HOTEL JORDAN
JERUSALEM-BIREH

PROFESSOR 1 (O.S.) (CONT'D)
There are moments of movement where you could add sound, break the silence, but it would ruin it.

STUDENT 1 (O.S.)
The silence worked for me, too. I can't really see it with sound.

PROFESSOR 1 (O.S.)
Anyway I think the major concern is the content. We've spent so much time thinking about this hotel business that we haven't focused on the raids, the military. This was a base! The Israelis were storming through these halls just a couple of years ago! Where is that?

STUDENT 2 (O.S.)
We have an interview with the guy who was here that night, but the audio isn't great.

PROFESSOR 2 (O.S.)
See, this is what I'm worried about.

The VISITOR finishes his sentence. It reads:

"no audio DUH - radio transmitter = IOF - more stories of occupied hotel, account of raid."

FADE TO:

INT. LAPTOP MONITOR - 10:10 AM

CALLER is humming as the Skype call rings. A phone number with an Israeli country code blinks in the center of the program window.

AUTOMATED RESPONSE 5
Thank you for calling Hilton Tel Aviv. Your call may be monitored for quality assurance purposes. Enjoy our luxurious rooms and suites. Each with a magnificent view of the Mediterranean. Relax in our premium Vista Lounge, and -

HILTON REP 1
Tel Aviv Hilton. Good afternoon, how may I help you?

CALLER
Hi there, I'm looking for some information about a Hilton hotel that may have existed outside of Jerusalem in the early '60s. I was wondering if there was, uh, anyone at your organization that I might be able to inquire about this with?

HILTON REP 1
We used to have one *in* Jerusalem. Right at the entrance.

CALLER
Right at the entrance to Jerusalem. Where exactly do you mean?

HILTON REP 1
Now it's the Crown Plaza Hotel.

CALLER
I see. This would've been a different building altogether. It was occupied by the military for a number of years, not far from where the Crown Plaza is now. You should have some record of it in your system.

HILTON REP 1
There were no other Hilton hotels near Jerusalem at that time, so there is no record. I'm not sure what story you've heard about the military -

CALLER
I'm quite certain. There must be a PR rep or someone I can speak with about this.

HILTON REP 1
Just a moment, sir.

AUTOMATED RESPONSE 5
- and gourmet dining. Try out our new Kosher sushi bar. *Be my guest at the Hilton.* Are you a member of our Hilton Honours? Earning both points and miles for stays around the world? Please inquire for details at the reception desk. Just sit back and enjoy your stay *at the Hilton. Be my guest at the Hilton.*
(MORE)

AUTOMATED RESPONSE 5 (CONT'D)

The Hilton Tel Aviv: Discovering the world of possibilities in the city that never sleeps. *Be my guest at the Hilton*. Enjoy our luxurious rooms and suites, each with a magnificent view of the Mediterranean. Relax in our premium Vista Lounge. Feel comfortable in the Executive Lounge. Take a dip in the pool, and rejuvenate yourself again under the sun. *Be my guest at the Hilton...* - and gourmet dining. Try out our new Kosher sushi bar. *Be my guest at the Hilton*. Are you a member of our Hilton Honours? Earning both points and miles for stays around the world? Please inquire for details at the reception desk. Just sit back and enjoy your stay *at the Hilton. Be my guest at the Hilton.* The Hilton Tel Aviv: Discovering the world of possibilities in the city that never sleeps. *Be my guest at the Hilton*. Enjoy our luxurious rooms and suites, each with a magnificent view of the Mediterranean. Relax in our premium Vista Lounge. Feel comfortable in the Executive Lounge. Take a dip in the pool, and rejuvenate yourself again under the sun. *Be my guest at the Hilton...* - and gourmet dining. Try out our new Kosher sushi bar. *Be my guest at the Hilton*. Are you a member of our Hilton Honours? Earning both points and miles for stays around the world? Please inquire for details at the reception desk. Just sit back and enjoy your stay *at the Hilton. Be my guest at the Hilton.* The Hilton Tel Aviv: Discovering the world of possibilities in the city that never sleeps. *Be my guest at the Hilton*. Enjoy our luxurious rooms and suites, each with a magnificent view of the Mediterranean. Relax in our premium Vista Lounge. Feel comfortable in the Executive Lounge. Take a dip in the pool, and rejuvenate yourself again under the sun. *Be my guest at the Hilton...* - and gourmet dining. Try out our new Kosher sushi bar.

(MORE)

AUTOMATED RESPONSE 5 (CONT'D)
Be my guest at the Hilton. Are you a member of our Hilton Honours? Earning both points and miles for stays around the world? Please inquire for details at the reception desk. Just sit back and enjoy your stay *at the* -

A click is heard and the call ends abruptly.

CUT TO BLACK.

.10

- وأطباقنا الراقية. جرّب مطبخ السوشي الكوشر الجديد. كن ضيفي في هيلتون. هل أنت عضو في هيلتون أونورز؟ لتكسب النقاط والأميال مقابل إقامتك لدينا حول العالم؟ للمزيد من التفاصيل يرجعى مكتب موظّف الإستقبال. ما عليك سوى الجلوس والراحة خلال زيارتك لـ هيلتون. كن ضيفي في هيلتون.
هيلتون تل أبيب: استكشف عالماً من الإمكانيات في المدينة التي لا تنام. كن ضيفي في هيلتون.
ستمتع بغرفنا وأجنحتنا الفخمة، كلّن بطلّة خلابة على البحر الأبيض المتوسط. استمتع بصالة فيستا الإستثنائية. استرخي في الصالة التنفيذية. إسبح وجدد شبابك تحت أشعة الشمس. كن ضيفي في هيلتون..–
- وأطباقنا الراقية. جرّب مطبخ السوشي الكوشر الجديد. كن ضيفي في هيلتون. هل أنت عضو في هيلتون أونورز؟ لتكسب النقاط والأميال مقابل إقامتك لدينا حول العالم؟ للمزيد من التفاصيل يرجعى مكتب موظّف الإستقبال. ما عليك سوى الجلوس والراحة خلال زيارتك لـ–

تسمع نقرة ويقطع الإتصال فجأة.

قطع إلى أسود.

HILTON HOTEL JORDAN JERUSALEM-BIREH

.9

المتصل
أنا متأكد من اللي بحكيلك
اياه. أكيد في موظف علاقات
عامة أو حدا ممكن أحكي معو
عن الموضوع.

موظف هيلتون 1
لحظة صغيرة أستاذي.

الرد الآلي 5
- وأطباقنا الراقية. جرّب مطبخ
السوشي الكوشر الجديد. كن ضيفي
ڤ هيلتون. هل أنت عضو في هيلتون
أونورز؟ لتكسب النقاط والأميال
مقابل إقامتك لدينا حول العالم؟
للمزيد من التفاصيل يرجعى
مكتب موظف الإستقبال. ما عليك
سوى الجلوس والراحة خلال زيارتك
لـــ هيلتون. كن ضيفي ڤ هيلتون.
هيلتون تل أبيب: استكشف عالما
من الإمكانيات في المدينة التي
لا تنام. كن ضيفي ڤ هيلتون.
ستمتع بغرفنا وأجنحتنا الفخمة،
كلّن بطلّة خلابة على البحر الأبيض
المتوسط. استمتع بصالة فيستا
الإستثنائية. استرخي في الصالة
التنفيذية. إسبح وجدد شبابك تحت
أشعة الشمس. كن ضيفي ڤ هيلتون...
- وأطباقنا الراقية. جرّب مطبخ
السوشي الكوشر الجديد. كن ضيفي
ڤ هيلتون. هل أنت عضو في هيلتون
أونورز؟ لتكسب النقاط والأميال
مقابل إقامتك لدينا حول العالم؟
للمزيد من التفاصيل يرجعى
مكتب موظف الإستقبال. ما عليك
سوى الجلوس والراحة خلال زيارتك
لـــ هيلتون. كن ضيفي ڤ هيلتون.
هيلتون تل أبيب: استكشف عالما
من الإمكانيات في المدينة التي
لا تنام. كن ضيفي ڤ هيلتون.
ستمتع بغرفنا وأجنحتنا الفخمة،
كلّن بطلّة خلابة على البحر الأبيض
المتوسط. استمتع بصالة فيستا
الإستثنائية. استرخي في الصالة
التنفيذية. إسبح وجدد شبابك تحت
أشعة الشمس. كن ضيفي ڤ هيلتون...

.8

Ref. :

Date

الرد الآلي 5
شكراً لإتصالك بهيلتون تل أبيب.
نود بأعلامكم بأنه سيتم تسجل
المكالمة لضمان حفظ الجودة.
إستمتع بغرفنا وأجنحتنا الفخمة،
كلّن بطلّة خلابة على البحر
الأبيض المتوسط. استمتع بصالة
فيستا الإستثنائية. استرخي-

موظف هيلتون 1
هلتون تل أبيب، صباح
الخير، كيف بقدر أساعدك؟

المتصل
مرحبا، انا بدوّر على معلومات
عن فندق هيلتون ممكن كان برّا
القدس بأوائل الستينات.
فـ كنت بتسائل ازا في، إيه،
أي حدا عنكم ممكن يفيدني
بشوية معلومات عنو؟

موظف هيلتون 1
كان عنا واحد ۋ القدس.
بالزبط ع مدخل المدينة.

المتصل
بالزبط على مدخل القدس.
وين بالزبط قصدك؟

موظف هيلتون 1
هلأ صار فندق الكراون بلازا

المتصل
آه. هاد مبني تاني. المبنى
اللي انا مهتم فيه كان محتل
من قبل الجيش لأكتر من سنة،
مش بعيد كتير من مكان
الكراون بلازا هلأ. المفروض
تلاقي عنّو ملف بالسجلات عندك.

موظف هيلتون 1
ما كان في ولا فندق هيلتون
بالمنطقة قريب عالقدس بهديك
الفترة، فـ ما في أي سجل.
مش متأكد أنا أي قصة انت
سمعت عن الجيش-

زالت مهمّة: فينيل كبيرة، النص على ورق الرق، ماذة ديجيتال في المصدر1."

البروفيسور 2 (خ.ش.)
اه اعتقد انو أصوات الكليّة مستعملة كتير. أنا كنت بحكي أكتر عن الفيديو التاني.

البروفيسور 1 (خ.ش.)
بختلف معك تماماً. الهدوء والمدة همّ اللي بخلّو الشغل زابط. في لحظات فيها حركة وين ممكن تضيف صوت لتكسر الصمت بس برأيي هاد الاشي بخرّبها.

الطالب 1 (خ.ش.)
الصمت زبط معي انا كمان. مش قادر أتخيّل الفيديو مع صوت.

البروفيسور 1 (خ.ش.)
على كل حال إحنا همّنا الأساسي هو المحتوى. قضينا وقت كتير نفكّر بالأوتيل كـ أوتيل بس ما فكرنا بإجتياح الجيش. هاد كان الاشي الأساسي! الاسرائيليين كانوا رايحيين جايين بالممرات هدول قبل سنتين بس! وين كل هاد؟

الطالب 2 (خ.ش.)
عنّا مقابلة مع الشب اللي بكون هون بالليل، بس الصوت مش كتير منيح.

البروفيسور 2 (خ.ش.)
شايف، هاد اللي انا خايف منو.

ينهي الزائر جملته. تقرأ كالتالي:

"لا صوت (به!)- جهاز البث اللاسلكي = الجيش الإسرائيلي- قصص أكتر عن الفندق المحتل، شهادات عن الإجتياح."

تلاشي إلى:

داخلي. شاشة كمبيوتر محمول- 10:10 صباحا

يهمهم المتصل فيما يقوم سكايب بالرنين. يومض رقم تيلفون بمفتاح دولة اسرائيلي في منتصف شاشة البرنامج.

.6

Ref. :

Date

داخلي. غرفة صف جامعية- 4:45 مساء

انتهى الصف للتو من مشاهدة مقاطع فيديو تم تحضيرها لمعرضهم التعاونيّ. نافذة البرنامج مفتوحة على الكمبيوتر المحمول الذي يأخد منه جهاز البروجكتور مصدره للصور. أعلى النافذة يقرأ: "VLC media player"؛ وتحتها مباشرةً، "IMM newcut"؛ وتحت ذلك، "tryptic 1." ينتقد الطلاب والبروفيسورين العمل، ويناقشون خططاً للمراجعة. مرةً أخرى، يقوم زائر بتسجيل الملاحظات بينما يجري النقاش.

صورة مقرّبة على الصورة المعروضة.

البروفيسور 2 (خ.ش.)
أظن إنو في كتير صور قويّة هون،
انا متأكد. المبنى جاي قدام
وبالنص، وعنّا صورة واضحة عن
تاريخو. بس مش عارف ازا بفيدنا
شغل أكتر على الصوت.

الطالب 2 (خ.ش.)
قصدك أصوات أكتر؟

البروفيسور 2 (خ.ش)
مش بس أصوات أكتر، بس مقاطع
صوت مسجلة بجودة عالية عشان
نشتغل فيها معا الفيديو.
الصمت إلو مكانو، بس اعتقد
انو بتكون إستراتيجية أقوى
إزا بنلاقي محلات نكسر فيها هاد الصمت.

الطالب 3 (خ.ش.)
بالنسبة للفيديو تبعي أنا
ما بدي أحط صوت أكتر من
اللي موجود أصلا. جرّبت أحط
مقطع صوت لكافيتيريا مليانة
وما زبط، فـ قررت إنو
أتركو زي ما هو.

صورة مقرّبة من دفتر

يخربش الزائر جملة بينما تكمل المجموعة نقاشها. ملاحظاته في أعلى الصفحة تقرأ:

"صلاح: قطع جامد، إعادة تصوير الممر بالعكس على منشفة. الكل يستعمل المصعد؛ تعبان. ميمو ضد الصوت الغريب في البداية- يجب أن تبقى. أنا: عدم التزامن جوهري، أكتر من شاشة. المادية ما

HILTON HOTEL JORDAN JERUSALEM-BIREH

.5

يقدّم لكم الوجبات طوال اليوم
بلمسات عالمية، بالإضافة إلى
طاولة بلياردو، مناظر خلابة،
وجبات خفيفة ومرطبات يوميًا
من الساعة الـ10 صباحا وحتى
الـ10 مساء. نتشرّف بزيارتكم
وجعل أوقاتكم لا تُنسى. للمزيد
من المعلومات والحجوزات،
اتصل على 96232093209.
أوعلىالبريد الإلكتروني:
doubletreeaqaba.info@hilton ...
مرحبا بك في دبل ثري هيلتون
العقبة. تبدأ ضيافتنا السخيّة
هنا بكعكة صغيرة برقائق
الشوكولاته لإعطائك إحساسا
حقيقي بالإهتمام والراحة.
يمكنك بالإضافة تدليل نفسك
في غرفنا الواسعة والفاخرة،
المفروشة بكل وسائل الراحة
للإستمتاع بيوم حصري. يقدّم
لك الطراز الإيطالي للفندق
غرفا وأجنحة مجهّزة تماما
لراحتك. إستمتع بمطاعمنا
وباراتنا المتنوعة. يقدّم
"جريل الملك" أرقى الستيك
والنبيذ من ال6:30 وحتى
الـ11 مساء. دي لاونج يقدّم
الأطعمة شهية من الـ10 مساء
وحتى الـ3 صباحا. جوستو،
يقدّم لكم الوجبات طوال اليوم
بلمسات عالمية، بالإضافة إلى
طاولة بلياردو، مناظر خلابة،
وجبات خفيفة ومرطبات يوميًا
من الساعة الـ10 صباحا وحتى
الـ10 مساء. نتشرّف بزيارتكم
وجعل أوقاتكم لا تُنسى. للمزيد
من المعلومات والحجوزات،
اتصل على 96232093209.
أوعلىالبريد الإلكتروني:
...doubletreeaqaba.info@hilton
مرحبا بك في دبل ثري هيلتون

تُسمع نقرة ويقطع الإتصال فجأة.

قطع إلى:

.4

Ref. :

Date

هنا بكعكة صغيرة برقائق
الشوكولاته لإعطائك إحساساً
حقيقي بالإهتمام والراحة.
يمكنك بالإضافة تدليل نفسك
في غرفنا الواسعة والفاخرة،
المفروشة بكل وسائل الراحة
للإستمتاع بيوم حصري. يقدّم
لك الطراز الإيطالي للفندق
غرفاً وأجنحة مجهّزة تماماً
لراحتك. إستمتع بمطاعمنا
وباراتنا المتنوعة. يقدّم
"جريل الملك" أرقى الستيك
والنبيذ من ال6:30 وحتى
الـ11 مساءً. دي لاونج يقدّم
الأطعمة شهية من الـ10 مساءً
وحتى الـ3 صباحاً. جوستو،
يقدّم لكم الوجبات طوال اليوم
بلمسات عالمية، بالإضافة إلى
طاولة بلياردو، مناظر خلابة،
وجبات خفيفة ومرطبات يوميًا
من الساعة الـ10 صباحاً وحتى
الـ10 مساءً. نتشرّف بزيارتكم
وجعل أوقاتكم لا تُنسى. للمزيد
من المعلومات والحجوزات،
اتصل على 96232093209.
أوعلىالبريدالإلكتروني:
...doubletreeaqaba.info@hilton
مرحبا بك في دبل تري هيتلون
العقبة. تبدأ ضيافتا الس
مرحباً بك في دبل ثري هيلتون
العقبة. تبدأ ضيافتنا السخيّة
هنا بكعكة صغيرة برقائق
الشوكولاته لإعطائك إحساساً
حقيقي بالإهتمام والراحة.
يمكنك بالإضافة تدليل نفسك
في غرفنا الواسعة والفاخرة،
المفروشة بكل وسائل الراحة
للإستمتاع بيوم حصري. يقدّم
لك الطراز الإيطالي للفندق
غرفاً وأجنحة مجهّزة تماما
لراحتك. إستمتع بمطاعمنا
وباراتنا المتنوعة. يقدّم
"جريل الملك" أرقى الستيك
والنبيذ من ال6:30 وحتى
الـ11 مساءً. دي لاونج يقدّم
الأطعمة شهية من الـ10 مساءً
وحتى الـ3 صباحاً. جوستو،

HILTON HOTEL JORDAN
JERUSALEM-BIREH

اشي فيه قصة جديدة، بس شكلو
كاين أوتيل عادي.

البروفيسور 1
كان في صور غير هدول في البيت.
غوشة ما خلاني استعير كل الصور
الموجودين عندو. راح أحاول أقنعو
يعطيني البقية، بس مش عارفة.
إزا لأ، الشغل بصير عن هاي الرقابة،
المعلومات الناقصة، والذاكرة المبنيّة.

ينهي الزائر جملته. تقرأ كالتالي:

"كلية تمريض، بناية زرقاء؟ الرقابة من غوشة، استعادة بقيّة الصور."

تلاشي إلى:

داخلي. شاشة كمبيوتر محمول- 12:10 ظهراً

يهمهم المتصل فيما يقوم سكايب بالرنين. يومض رقم تيلفون بمفتاح دولة الأردن في منتصف شاشة البرنامج.

ممثل دبل تري 1
شكراً لإتصالك بدبل تري العقبة،
عمر معك، كيف ممكن أساعدك؟

المتصل
مرحبا عمر. أنا باحث وعم بحاول
ألاقي معلومات عن تاريخ فندق
هيلتون انبنى في المنطقة في،
إيه، أوائل الستينات، ويا ريت
لو تقدر تحولني ع موظّف علاقات
عامة أو أي حدا عندو-

ممثل دبل تري 1
(مقاطعاً)
لحظة، راح أحول لمسؤول
العلاقات، إيه، العامة

المتصل
شكراً كتير.

الرد الآلي 4
مرحباً بك في دبل تري هيتلون
العقبة. تبدأ ضيافتا الس
مرحباً بك في دبل ثري هيلتون
العقبة. تبدأ ضيافتنا السخيّة

.2

على شوية معلومات بخصوص أوتيل
من فروعكم يمكن كان موجود
بالقدس بالستينات. ممكن
لو سمعت، ايه، ترجعلي بإيميل،
مم، بكون ممنونلك...

يخفت صوت المتصل وينتهي الإتصال. يهمهم الآن بسرعة أكبر.

قطع إلى:

داخلي. غرفة صف جامعية- 4:30 مساء
صف صغير يتجمّع حول طاولة مغطية بالوثائق. موضوع المحادثة هو المبنى الذي يجلسون فيه، ويتنازعون حول التاريخ الذي يحوم حول المبنى. البروفيسور الأول يرأس النقاش مع الطلاب الأربعة فيما يقوم البروفيسور 2 بإيجاد صورة على الكمبيوتر المحمول ليشاركها مع المجموعة. يقوم زائر بمعاينة النقاش وتسجيل الملاحظات.

صورة جوية للطاولة

الطالب 1
انا حكيت مع مرة اشتغلك هون
لما كان المبنى كليّة للتمريض.
هي ما بتعرف كتير عن الأوتيل
بس عندها قصص كتير عن الكليّة.
وشكلو المبنى كاين مدهون بلون
أزرق من برا.

البروفيسور 1
همم. بكون رائع لو نلاقي صورة
من هداك الوقت. شو رأيك بالصور
اللي ورجانا اياهم غوشة؟

صورة مقرّبة من دفتر

يخربش الزائر جملة بينما تكمل المجموعة نقاشها. ملاحظاته في أعلى الصفحة تقرأ:

"غوشة قرض لمستشفى 61. البنك يرفض فكرة مستشفى > يطلب أوتيل > افتتاح الكارلتون بزواج غوشة 1962. يصبح هيلتون بال63 (ليش؟ مسجل كارلتون/هيلتون؟) يقتحم الإحتلال المبنى بال67، يسرقون لوحة هلتون، يتحول لمعسكر جيش (على تلّة مرتفعة) حتى سنة 70. تتغير الملكية، قس أرمني ومنظّمة استيطانية (!) لها حصّة > تتدخل منظمة التحرير في أواخر ال70 وتتملّك المبنة"

الطالب 2 (غ.ش.)
وثائق الأوتيل مثيرة للإهتمام
بس الصور عاديين. وأنا
بعمللهم سكان كنت حابب ألاقي

HILTON HOTEL JORDAN
JERUSALEM-BIREH

داخلي. شاشة كمبيوتر محمول- 12:02 ظهراً

برنامج "سكايب" على الشاشة ونسمع صوت بداية الرنين. ينقر المتصل على أزرار الكمبيوتر وصوته على الجهاز مسموع جيداً في إنتظار المكالمة القادمة. في حين إنتظار الرد، يهمهم المتصل نغمة رباعيّة النوتات. الصوت الآخر يأتي من خلال السماعات بشكل مشوّش ولكن مسوع.

ترّرن ترّرن ترّر

الرد الآلي 1 (خ.ش.)
هيلتون...

المتصل (خ.ش.)
آلو؟

الرد الآلي 1 (خ.ش.)
(باستعجال)
نعتذر، البريد الصوتي ممتلئ.
لا تستطيع ترك رسالة لهذا المستخدم.
تستطيع إنهاء المكالمة الآن أو
إدخال امتداد آخر.

المتصل (خ.ش.)
يلعن...

يحوم مؤشر الفأرة فوق أيقونة الهاتف الحمراء. نسمع صوت نقرة، وينتهي الإتصال. المزيد من النقر والهمهمة. يُسمع صوت خرخشة مجدداً ويبدأ الرنين مجدداً.

الرد الآلي 2 (خ.ش.)
هيلتون العالمية-

الرد الآلي 3 (خ.ش.)
- غير متوفرة. قم بتسجيلرسالتك
بعد سماع الرنين. عند الإنتهاء
من تسجيل رسالتك قم بإنهاء
المكالمة أو الضغط على الرقم
1 للمزيد من الخيارات.

بيب

المتصل (خ.ش.)
مم، مرحبا. ايه، انا بدوّر

CARLTON HOTEL

RAMALLAH — JERUSALEM

Tel. 293 RAMALLAH
352 JERUSALEM

P. O. B. RAMALLAH

P. O. B. 35 JERUSALEM

ندق كارلتون

رام الله – القدس

تلفون ٢٩٣ رام الله
٣٥٢ القدس

صندوق البريد رام الله

صندوق البريد ٣٥ القدس

مقتطفات من مبنى قيد الإنشاء

كتبه
CAJ

ترجمة
فادي أبو نعمة
صلاح شباك

11شارع الياسمين، القدس/البيرة/رام الله
054/056/0599309106

كارلتون في تل أبيب، صادر الجنود الإسرائيليون يافطة هيلتون من مبنى غوشة. وفي أوائل السبعينيات، استخدمه الجيش الإسرائيلي كقاعدة له. مؤخراً، حولته جامعة القدس إلى سكن للإناث تابع لكلية التمريض، واستمر كذلك إلى أن ظهرت محطة تلفزيونية أهلية في المكان عام ١٩٩٦، وفيها أنتجت نسخة عربية من برنامج شارع سمسم. وفي زمن قريب، صادر الجيش الإسرائيلي أجهزة البث وأغلق المحطة التي أدارها الأهالي، والذين تحولوا بدورهم للبث عبر اليوتيوب وقنوات أخرى تحت اسم «هنا القدس».

يسار والصفحات التالية:
نص فيلم من إنتاج كيسي آسبروث-جاكسون (٢٠١٤)، بالتعاون مع فادي أبونعمة وصلاح شباك عن المبنى، وهو الآن مقر معهد الإعلام العصري في جامعة القدس

يخبرني فؤاد الصايغ بأن مكتبه احترق أيام أحداث أيلول الأسود في الأردن. كل الصور الأصلية والمخططات ورسومات أعماله الأولى لم تعد موجودة. هنالك بعض الصور الفوتوغرافية التي تحتفظ ابنته (وهي معمارية أيضاً) بنسخ رقمية منها. يتذكر الصايغ أنه صمم أربعة مبانٍ في فلسطين وكلها قبل ١٩٦٧؛ واحد منها هو مبنى مكتب البريد في شارع صلاح الدين بالقدس. اشترت شركة عقارية تدعى عطيرت كوهانيم طابقاً من ذلك المبنى مؤخراً لتسكن فيه مدرسة دينية يهودية متشددة، من أهدافها أن يصبح اليهود أغلبية في القدس الشرقية. لم يعرف الصايغ هذا الأمر وقتها.

المبنى الثاني كان فندق هيلتون كارلتون بين رام الله والقدس. بناه صاحبه محمد جودت غوشة أصلاً كمستشفى من واجهتين. صمم عام ١٩٥٩ وافتتح عام ١٩٦٣. كان قد تخرج الصايغ حديثاً من القاهرة وقتها، ويبدو أنه أراد مبنى غير مرتبط بحقبة تاريخية قدر الإمكان في تصميمه النهائي: خطوط هندسية نظيفة وخرسانة مسلحة مقصوصة بشكل واضح وواجهة ذات لون وردي باهت على جانبها. عندما افتتح هيلتون

فؤاد الصايغ،
رغم ذلك

Sayed Karim, Baba Pink

The Egyptian architect Sayed Karim began designing this residence for Abdel Moti Qutob in Beit Hanina, Jerusalem, in 1959. Burgundy mosaic and aluminum were apparently flown in from Italy. It was complete in 1963. By the time the Qutobs moved in, demonstrations against the government had broken out, protesting the implementation of student identity cards. The architect Rizek Khoury was building a house up the hill from the Qutobs' for King Hussein. According to Khaled Qutob, the king, who was looking to have more of his presence felt on the West Bank, was walking by, fell in love with their residence, and requested to rent it while his palace up the hill was being constructed. Abdel Moti Qutob was the head of the former Air Jordan before the king had dissolved the company to make way for Alia (now Royal Jordanian).

Qutob moved out and agreed to rent his home to King Hussein—probably, according to Khaled Qutob, as a gesture to show that he was a man who never bears professional grudges, according to his son. The 1967 war broke out, the West Bank, East Jerusalem, Gaza, and the Golan Heights were annexed to the rest of Israel, and the palace was never completed. Nevertheless, the Qutobs moved back in and thrived in its rectilinear spaces.

Sayed Karim was an instrumental figure in regional and national Egyptian architectural modernism. His work was critically fed, and spread, through his magazine *al-'Imara*, first published in 1939. His polemics are most evident in 1945, when, according to Mohamed Elshahed's brilliant excavations of his works, Karim published a provocative illustration and article titled "If Cairo Were Destroyed!" in the magazine *Al-Ithnayn wal-Dunya*, where he writes, "World architects are busy designing the reconstruction of cities destroyed in the war [...]. If we had the opportunity to destroy Cairo and rebuild it, where would we begin and what would we do?"[21]

21 Sayed Karim, quoted in Elshahed, "Revolutionary Modernism?," 140.

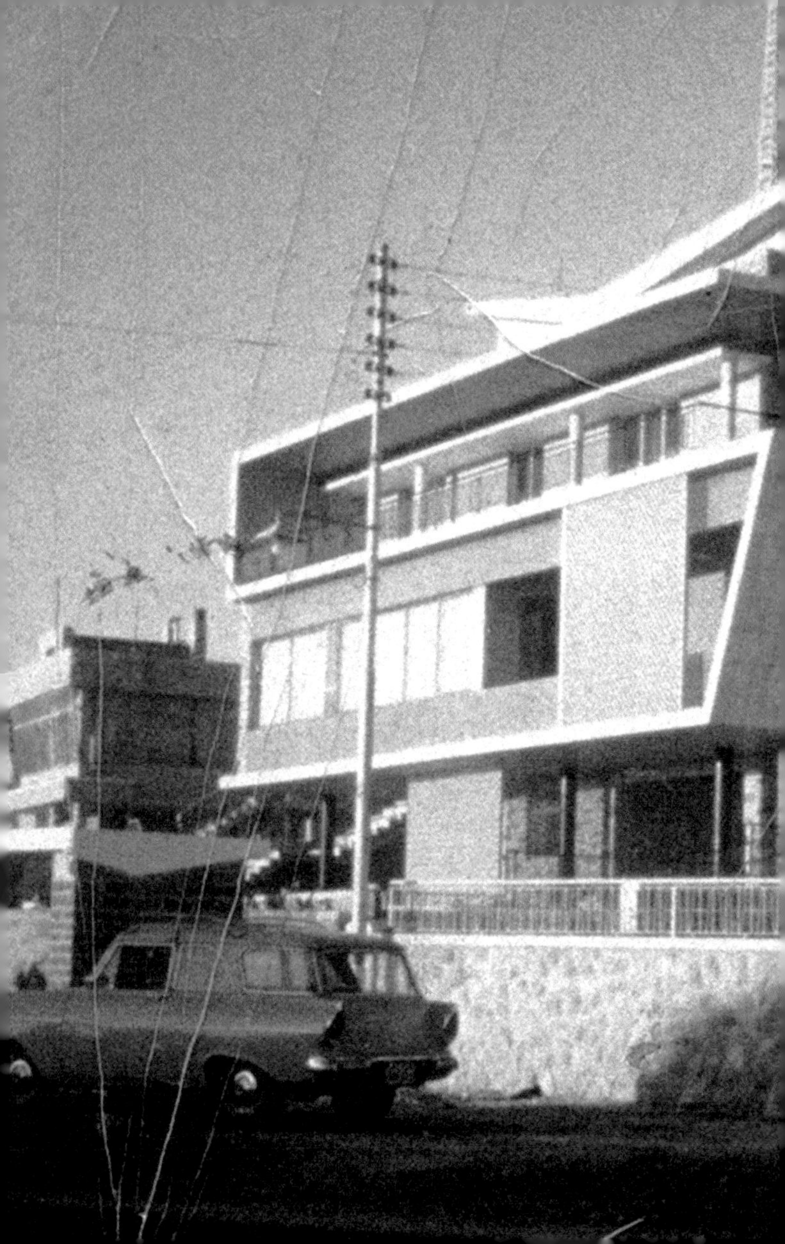

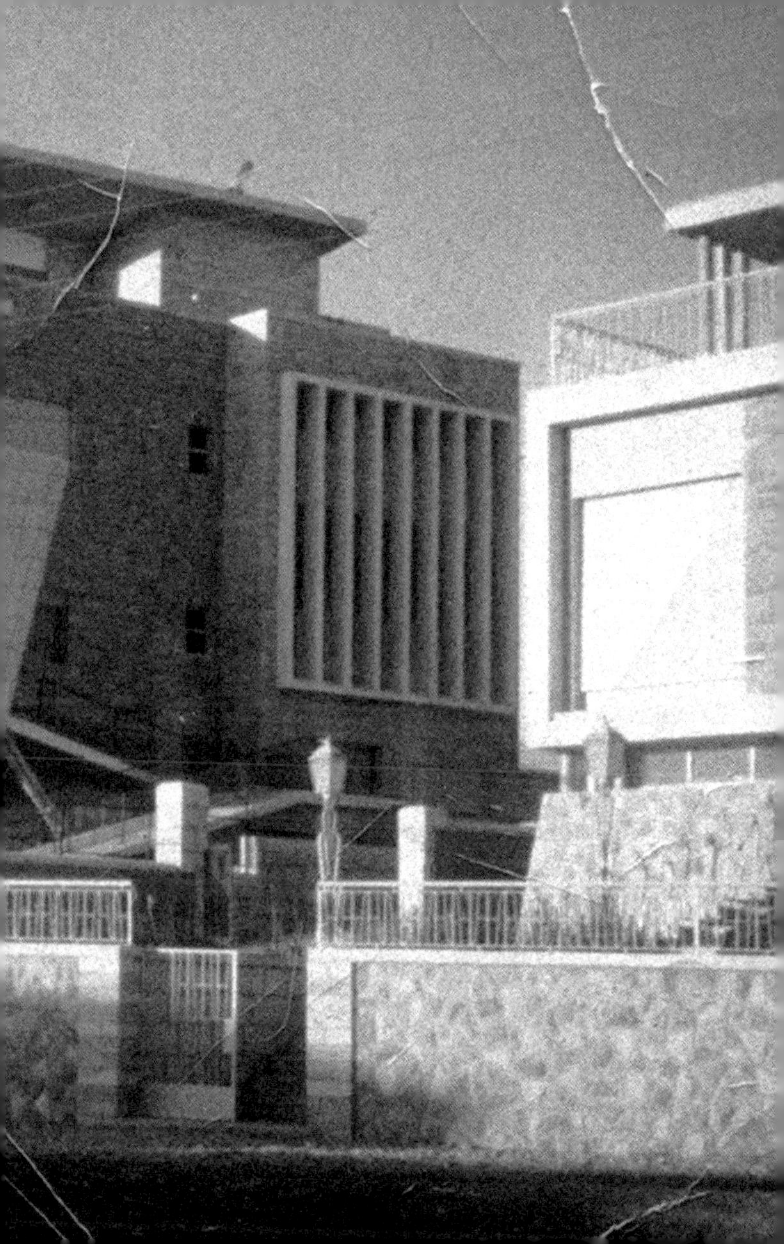

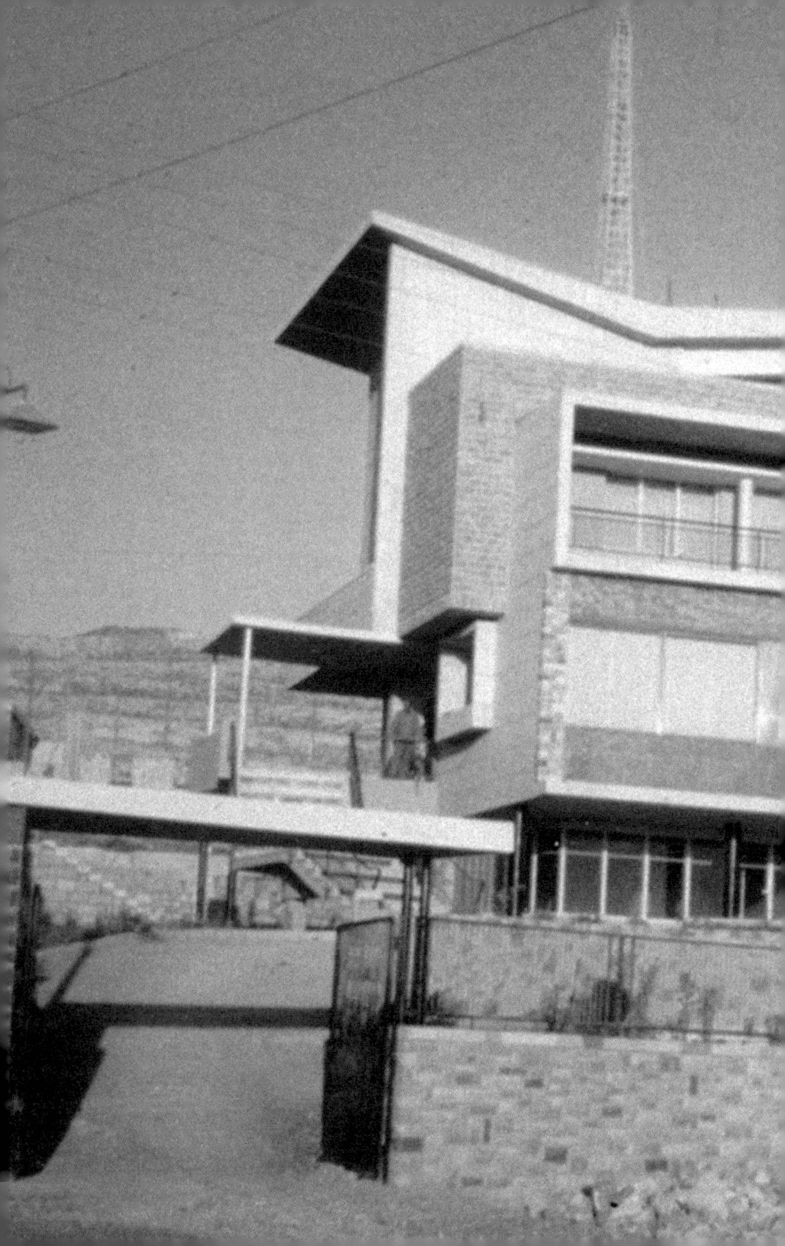

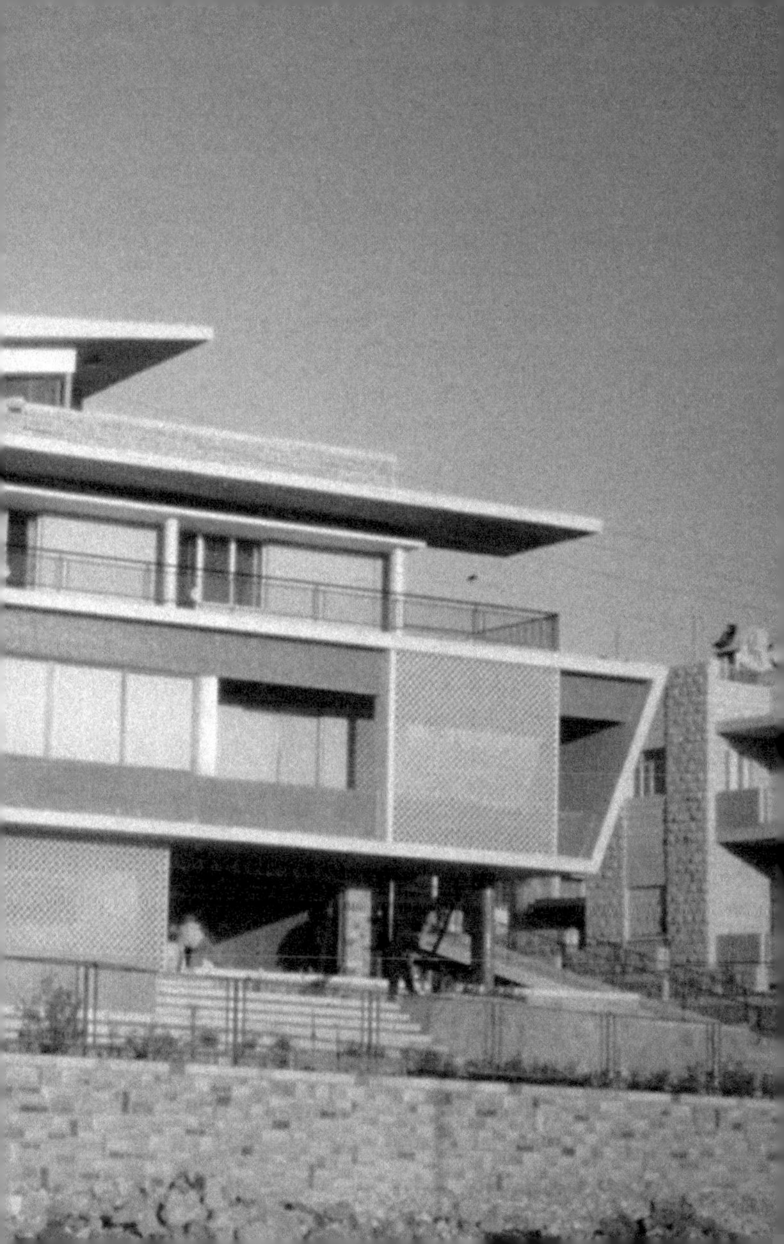

عادت عائلة القطب لتسكن منزلها وتستمع بخطوطه المستقيمة.

كان للمعماري سيد كريم أثر كبير في الحداثة المعمارية في مصر والمنطقة. رفد أعماله بنشرها في مجلته «العمارة» التي أسسها عام ١٩٣٩. بحسب دراسة محمد الشاهد التي بحثت في أعماله، تجلت نظريات كريم عام ١٩٤٥ عندما نشر تصوراً مرسوماً ومقالة عنوانها «لو هدمت القاهرة!» في مجلة «الإثنين والدنيا». كتب كريم في المقالة «نشط المهندسون العالميون في وضع مشاريع تعمير العواصم التي دمرتها الحرب... فلو تيسر لنا هدم القاهرة وإعادة بنائها... فأين نبدأ أو كيف ننتهي؟»[٢١]

٢١ سيد كريم، اقتباس في مقالة الشاهد «حداثة ثورية؟»، ١٤٠.

بدأ المعماري المصري سيد كريم بتصميم مسكن عبدالمعطي القطب في بيت حنينا بالقدس عام ١٩٥٩. استورد بلاط الموزاييك الخمري والألمنيوم بالطائرة من إيطاليا. اكتمل بناؤه عام ١٩٦٣، وعندما انتقلت عائلة القطب للسكن فيه، اندلعت مظاهرات ضد الحكومة اعترضت على تطبيق تعليمات متعلقة باستصدار بطاقات هوية للطلاب. كان المعماري رزق خوري يبني بيتاً للملك حسين على التلة المجاورة لبيت القطب. طبقاً لرواية عائلة القطب، كان الملك يتمشى في المنطقة عندما وقع في حب منزلهم وطلب أن يستأجره إلى أن ينتهي البناء في قصره على أعلى التل. كان عبدالمعطي القطب رئيس شركة الطيران الأردني والتي حلها الملك حسين ليفسح المجال لشركة عالية (الملكية الأردنية الآن). وافق القطب على تأجير المنزل وانتقل منه لصالح الملك، ربما ليثبت أنه لا يحمل ضغينة مهنية، بحسب ما يعتقد ابنه الآن. عندما اندلعت حرب ١٩٦٧، سيطرت إسرائيل على الضفة الغربية والقدس الشرقية وغزة ومرتفعات الجولان. ورغم أن القصر لم يكتمل بناؤه،

سيد كريم،

بابا زهري

Jafar Tukan,
Fly Away Home

Jafar Tukan's first cantilever was commissioned by his uncle Mohammad Zeid al-Kilani in Nablus and, like many structures at the time, was constructed by a builders cooperative of women and men. Tukan had just graduated from the American University of Beirut in 1960 and managed to complete the project by 1963. When the concrete cantilever was raised, the joke in Nablus was that it was going to fall on someone's head. Around fifty years later, Kilani's son repainted the cantilever, because it had turned slightly gray over the years. The paint peeled shortly thereafter. Through the years, due to changing circumstances, various modifications were made to the house. So much so, that Jafar Tukan would joke, "One dares to say I built this."

Like many residents of the old city, Jafar's aunt, the poet and writer Fadwa Toukan, left the family home in the old city, a traditional courtyard-type house cooled by fountains and plants, for a quiet basement garden extension at the Kilanis' (Mohammad was her brother-in-law).[22] Fadwa went to a blacksmith to design a metal door for the entrance. The blacksmith returned with her design as requested, with one addition—he wanted to surprise and honor her with the Latin letter *F* (for Fadwa) in the middle of the ironwork. But it had been inserted the wrong way around. Fadwa left it as it was, and could not thank him enough for it.

Jafar went on to design multiple projects in Beirut and then, after the civil war, settled in Amman. He continued to roam the area as if it were still one neighborhood; one could find him on Hamra Street in Beirut eating a falafel, then dining at Jabri Restaurant in Damascus, and then at an opening in Darat al Funun in Amman. In 2005 he designed the Yasser Arafat Mausoleum, covered entirely in modernist tropes. He died in 2014 after a long battle with multiple sclerosis.

22 See Diala Khasawneh, *Palestinian Urban Mansions: Memoirs Engraved in Stone* (Ramallah: Riwaq–Centre for Architectural Conservation, 2001), especially her references to the population flux in Nablus's old city due to continued Israeli military operations in the city center. Refer also to Eyal Weizman's various studies on the Israeli Army's tactic of moving through the walls of Nablus's casbah (old city): "Walking Through Walls," *Transversal,* May 2007, http://eipcp.net/transversal/0507/weizman/en/.

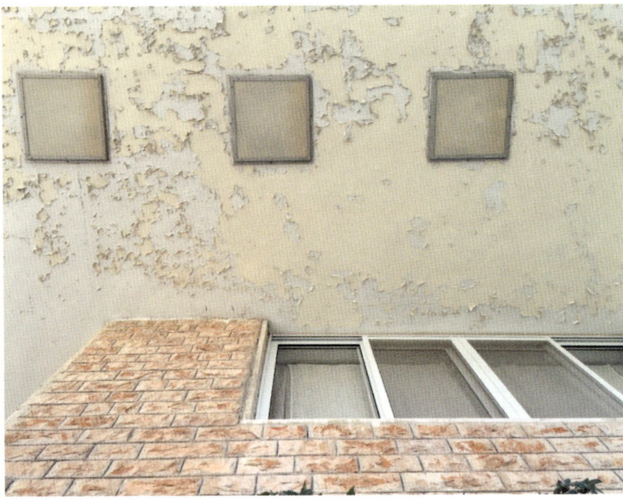

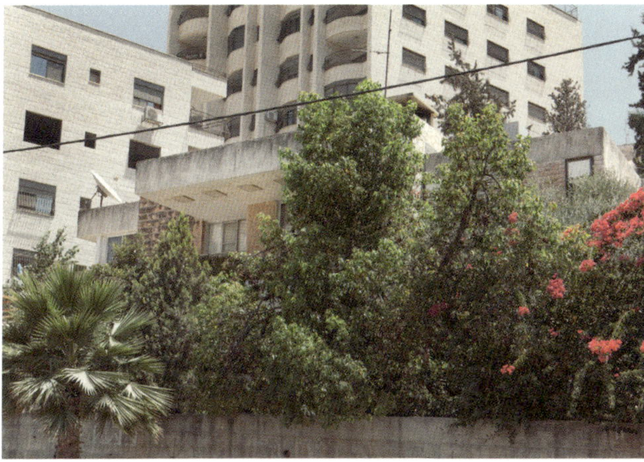

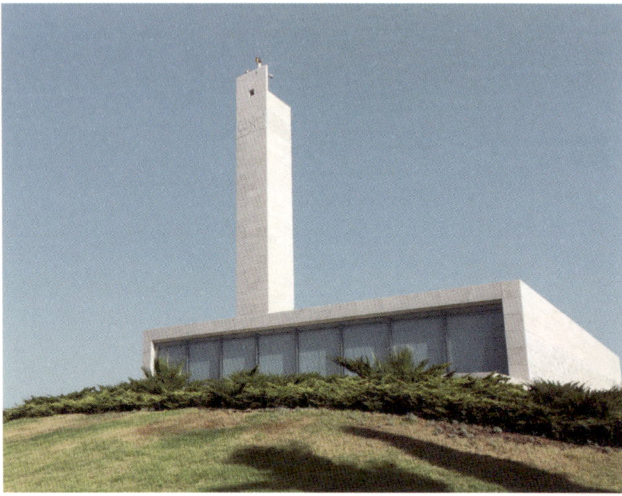

واحدا. أراد أن يفاجئها فوضع الحرف اللاتيني F، وهو الحرف الأول من اسمها، في وسط الباب الحديدي، إلا أنه وضعه مقلوبا. تركته فدوى كما كان ولم تكن تقدر على أن توفيه شكراً على صنيعه هذا.

استمر جعفر في تصميم مشاريع مختلفة في بيروت، وانتقل بعد الحرب الأهلية ليستقر في عمان. وظل يسافر في المنطقة كما لو أنها كلها حي واحد؛ فكان بالإمكان أن تراه يأكل الفلافل في شارع الحمرا ببيروت، ثم يتعشى في مطعم جبري بدمشق، ثم في افتتاح في دارة الفنون بعمان. عام ٢٠٠٥، صمم ضريح ياسر عرفات (صفحة ٢١٠) والذي غطي بشكل عام بتفاصيل معمارية حداثية. توفي عام ٢٠١٤ بعد صراع طويل مع مرض التصلب اللويحي.

٢٢ انظر كتاب ديالا خصاونة، «بيوت فلسطين: ذاكرة منحوتة في الحجر» (رام الله: رواق مركز المعمار الشعبي، ٢٠٠١)، خاصة في إشارتها إلى الدفق السكاني في نابلس القديمة نتيجة عمليات الجيش الإسرائيلي في وسط المدينة. كذلك انظر دراسات إيال وايزمان المختلفة عن أسلوب الجيش الإسرائيلي في المرور عبر جدران حي القصبة (في نابلس القديمة):

Diala Khasawneh, *Palestinian Urban Mansions: Memoirs Engraved in Stone* (Ramallah: Riwaq–Centre for Architectural Conservation, 2001).

"Walking Through Walls," *Transversal*, May 2007, http://eipcp.net/transversal/0507/weizman/en/.

مظلة جعفر طوقان الحرة الأولى. كلفه بتصميمها عمه محمد زيد الكيلاني في نابلس، وككثير من الأبنية في ذلك الوقت، بنتها تعاونية من النساء والرجال. كان طوقان قد تخرج من الجامعة الأمريكية في بيروت عام ١٩٦٠، وانتهى من هذا المشروع بحلول عام ١٩٦٣. عندما رفعت المظلة الناتئة، تناولها أهل نابلس بالنكتة وتوقعوا أن تقع على رأس أحدهم. بعد خمسين عاماً، قام ابن الكيلاني بإعادة دهان المظلة لأنها أصبحت رمادية اللون مع الزمن، ليتقشر الدهان بعدها بوقت قصير. طرأت تغييرات مختلفة على هذا المبنى نتيجة تغير الظروف. كانت كثيرة لدرجة أن جعفر طوقان قال مازحاً: «الواحد ما بسترجي يقول إني بنيت هذا المبنى.»

وككثير من سكان البلدة القديمة، تركت عمة جعفر، الشاعرة والكاتبة فدوى طوقان، بيت العائلة في البلدة القديمة وهو بيت تقليدي له فناء داخلي تحييه نوافير الماء والنباتات، لتستقر في طابق تسوية مطل على حديقة تابعة لبيت الكيلاني وعديله. طلبت فدوى من حداد أن يصنع لها باباً حديدياً للمدخل، وعاد الحداد بدوره بالتصميم المطلوب وقد أضاف إلى وسطه شيئا

جعفر طوقان،
البيت الطائر

Rizek Khoury, Foliage and Other Things

Rizek Khoury (also known as Abu Spiro), told me has no drawings from the earlier part of his career. In 1967, his office on top of Rukab's Ice Cream parlor was raided by the Israeli army. Khoury was one of the founders of the Palestinian architects' union and a full-time employee of the Ramallah Municipality. His private commissions include Hanan Ashrawi's residence, originally designed for her father Daoud Mikhail. He also designed Mustafa Dajani's villa in Jerusalem and the Atallah villa in al-Shayyah.

Muntazah Ramallah is the work I wish to focus on here: once a thriving public square in the garden of the municipality with a playground and restaurant, all revolving around a blue mosaic water fountain. Shade was provided by white, fanlike slabs of concrete that sat on steel cylinders, simply filled with cement and painted in glossy primary colors. Upon completion of the project in 1962, Abu Spiro drove a pick-up truck to Jenin and bought four star pine trees to plant in the space.[23] Abu Spiro was interested in their solid form and highly symmetrical branches—in his words, very much like a Christmas tree and somewhat reminiscent of Beirut. This pine reaches the height of its maturity at fifty to sixty years and then entirely loses its symmetry. In the summer of 2015, the municipality began to renovate the building and blatantly chopped down one of these trees—precisely at the height of its maturity—in the process.

Abu Spiro was emotional when he learned about this and the fact that they were also pulling apart the public grounds he once designed. He was *not* emotional in the least, however, when I mentioned they were also adding extensions and changing the facade of the building itself that he helped engineer. Buildings change.

Coinciding exactly with this destruction, it was decided by the Nablus Municipality that an abandoned villa designed by Hani Arafat would also be torn down, as well as the midcentury cinema Al-Assi. But unlike these buildings, the municipal grounds represented one of the few examples where the social potential of modernist planning found expression through its open, accessible, rational design—not merely as a stylistic influence. Charles Kidess, an architect currently producing a handful of appealingly clean, glossy lines in al-Tireh, Ramallah, envisioned this "rehabilitation" project since as far back as the mid 1990s, when he first arrived from Australia. As he put it: "I wanted to create a public space." But the square was already a public space, long before they bulldozed parts of it: a place were families smoked *argilleh* while children played on coin-operated dolphin rides synced to Nancy Ajram's music. It seems they wanted a different kind of public. Renditions of their proposal collage Angelina Jolie into the new municipality grounds with her son Maddox in one part of the image, and walking her dog in another.

The enormous condescension of these makeovers is most striking. This renovation could be seen as the exact point at which a mirror was held up to the Palestinian Authority, so that it might confront its own view of the world and its approach to urban development in the last decade. In Yazid Anani's words, a neocolonial era that has "transform[ed] the long history of political resistance and struggle against occupation into a neoliberal project, to the point of presenting itself as the project for achieving the Palestinian dream"[24]—the figure of Angelina Jolie, here, being the culmination of such a dream. For a course I cotaught with

Anani on the archive, the students excavated a digital file of past incursions on that same building by the Israeli Army. In a photo taken after a 2002 incursion, one of the pine trees is framed by the large, glass windows of the municipality, while a framed map of historic Palestine is left intact on the wall.

23 Incidentally, star pines are also native to Norfolk Island, and were said to be an initial lure—timber for shipbuilding—for the British when settling the island.

24 Yazid Anani, "Academia, The Mirror" (lecture, Designing Civic Encounter Symposium, ArtTerritories, Ramallah, July 2011), http://www.artterritories.net/designingcivicencounter/?page_id=13.

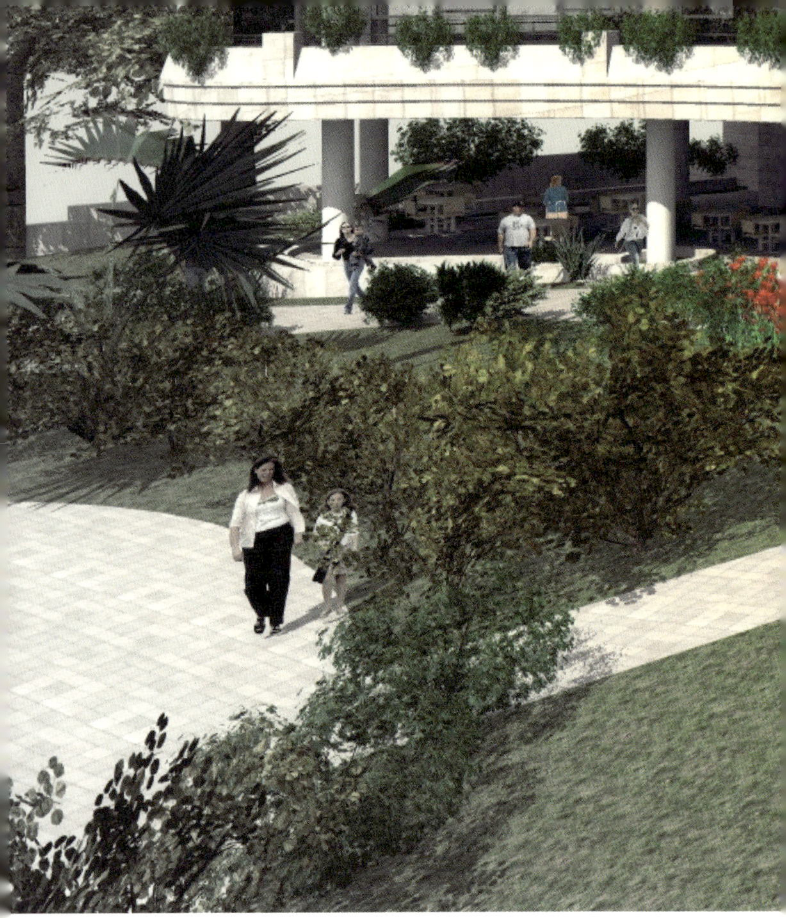

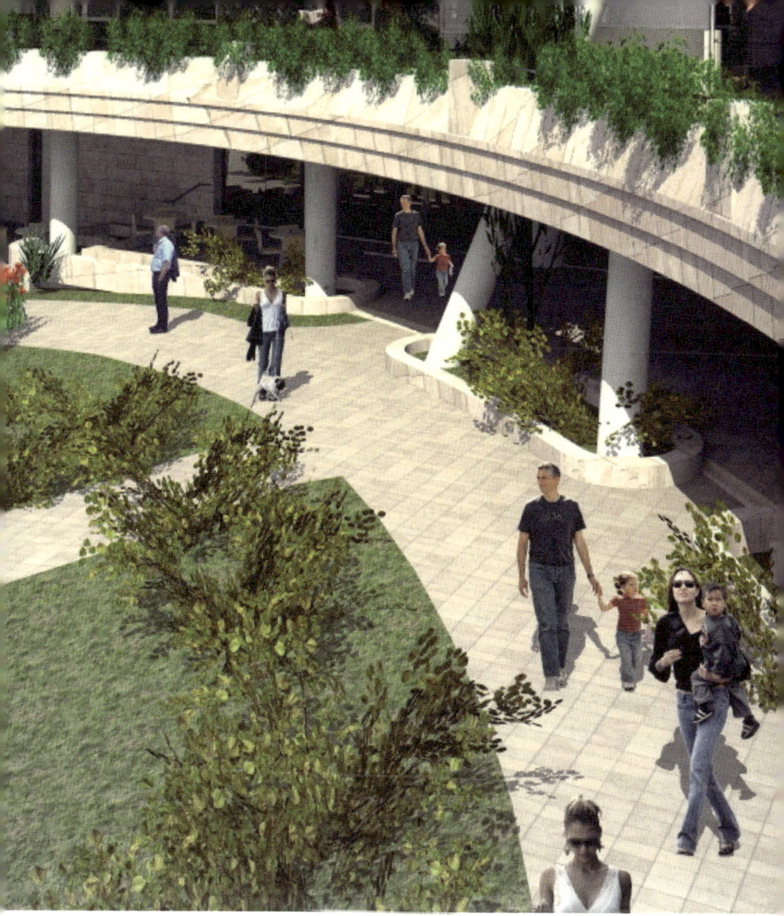

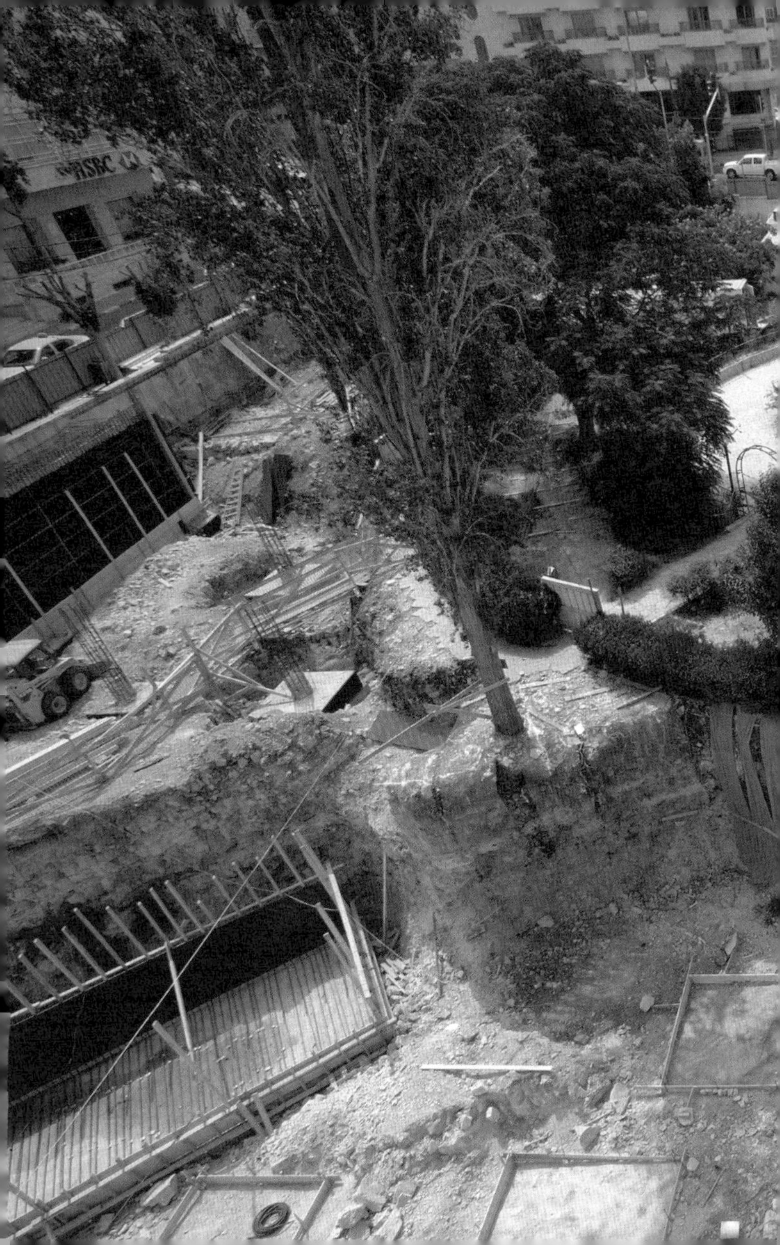
HSBC

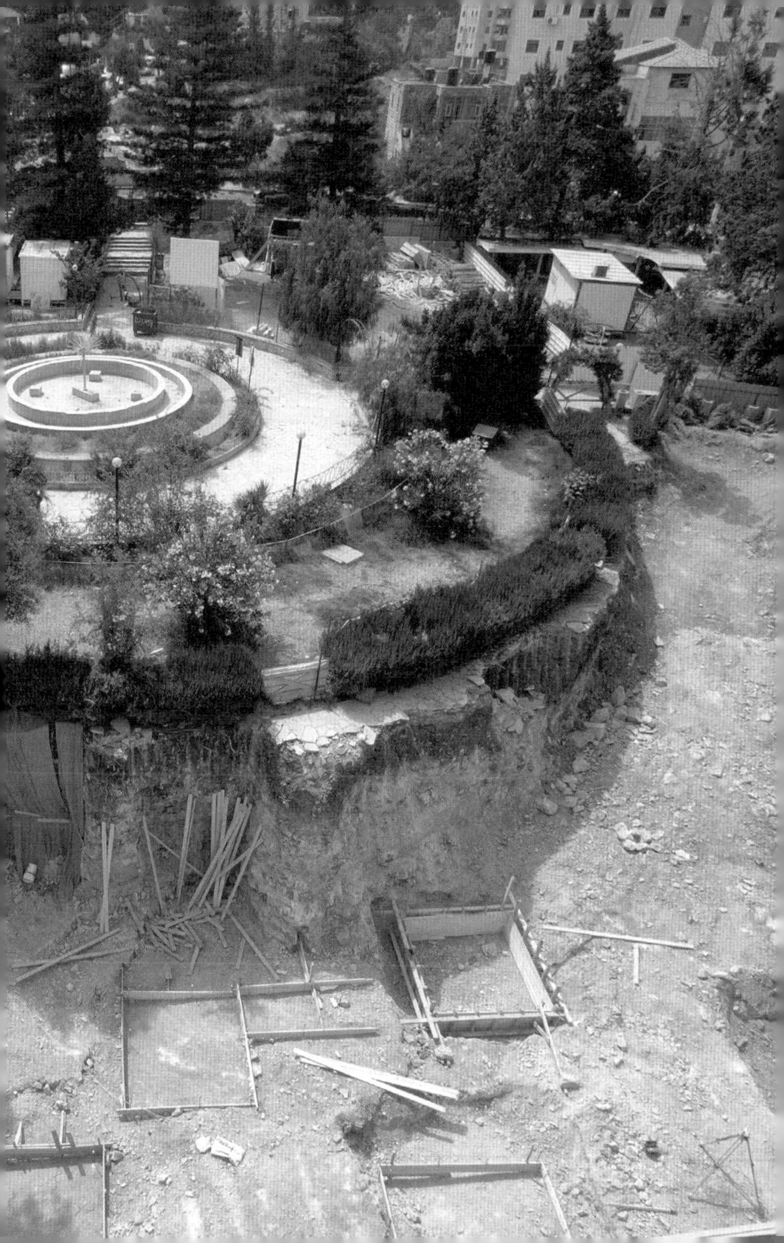

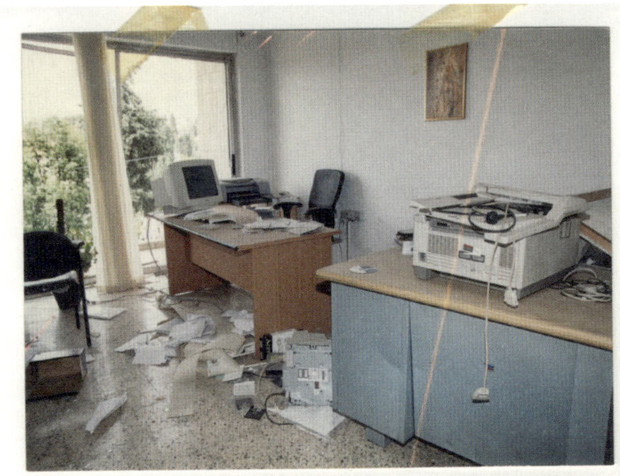

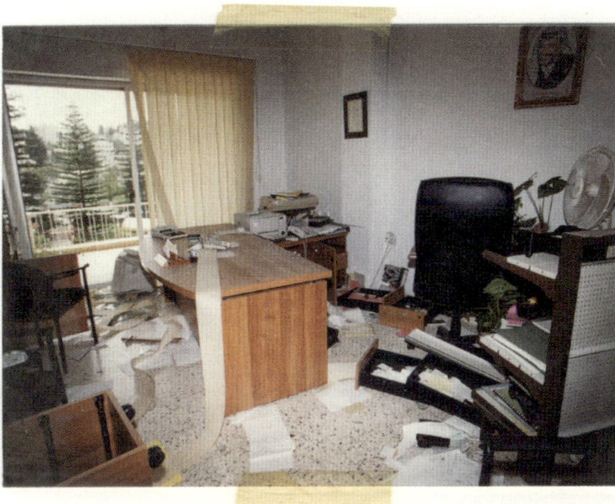

Amara architects

Like This Page · February 2014 ·

Ramallah Municipality is reaching out for the public. With the creation of public plaza, it is inviting people to come and participate in day to day activities. — in Ramallah.

Amara architects We tried to create a touch of monumentality for a municipality building in an otherwise modern, green, open and transparent composition

1 · February 25, 2014 at 12:45am

للحلم. وفي مساق قمت بتدريسه مع عناني عن الأرشيف، بحث الطلاب في ملفات رقمية عن مداهمات سابقة تعرض لها هذا المبنى من قبل الجيش الإسرائيلي. وجدت صورة أخذت بعد اقتحام حصل عام ٢٠٠٢، تحولت واحدة من شجرات الصنوبر إلى صورة في إطار نافذة من غرفة في مبنى البلدية، بينما ظلت خريطة فلسطين التاريخية سليمة دون أذى في إطارها على الحائط.

٢٣ للصدفة، شجرة الصنوبر هذه أصلها جزيرة نورفولك، ويقال إنها أول الأخشاب التي استخدمت في بناء السفن، تحديداً للبريطانيين الذين استقروا على هذه الجزيرة.

يسار:
مكتب عمارة: بلدية رام الله تتواصل مع الجمهور. بخلق هذه الساحة العامة، تدعو البلدية الناس إلى زيارة الساحة والمشاركة في نشاطاتها اليومية.

مكتب عمارة: نحاول أن نضفي لمسة من الضخامة لمبنى البلدية في تنسيق حديث أخضر منفتح وشفاف.

التأهيل التي ظهرت أواسط التسعينيات، وذلك عندما عاد من أستراليا. يقول: «أردت أن أصنع فضاءً عاماً.» لكن المنتزه كان فضاءً عاماً بزمن سبق عمليات الإزالة التي مست أجزاءً منه: كان مكاناً تدخن فيه العائلات الأرجيلة بينما يلعب أطفالهم على دلافين تعمل بالقطع النقدية لتتراقص على نغم أغاني نانسي عجرم. يبدو أنهم أرادوا نوعاً مختلفاً من الجمهور. الصور المركبة على الكمبيوتر تضع أنجلينا جولي في منتزه البلدية الجديد، مع ابنها مادوكس في جزء من الصورة، وتتمشى مع كلبها في جزء آخر.

إن التباهي الضخم الذي تصنعه هذه التجديدات هو الأكثر لفتاً للنظر. يمكن لهذا الترميم أن يُرى كأنه نفس النقطة التي تسلط فيه مرآة على السلطة الفلسطينية لتستطيع أن تفهم رؤيتها للعام ونهجها في التخطيط الحضري في العقد الفائت. يقول يزيد عناني إن حقبة استعمارية جديدة «حولت التاريخ الطويل للمقاومة السياسية والنضال ضد الاحتلال إلى مشروع نيوليبرالي يقدّم نفسه على أنه المشروع المناسب لتحقيق الحلم الفلسطيني». شخصية أنجلينا جولي هنا، هي تكثيف

وتذكره بشكل ما ببيروت. تصل هذه الأشجار أوجها على عامها الخمسين أو الستين ثم تفقد من بعدها التناظر أو التماثل بين فروعها. في صيف ٢٠١٥، بدأت البلدية بترميم المبنى ولتحقق ذلك قامت بقطع واحدة من هذه الأشجار، الآن، وهي في أوجها.

تأثر أبو سبيرو عندما علم بصنيع البلدية وعندما علم أنهم سيزيلون الملاعب العامة التي صممها فيما مضى. لكنه لم يتأثر عندما ذكرت له أنهم يخططون لإضافة عناصر جديدة وسيغيرون شكل واجهة المبنى نفسه الذي ساهم في تعميره. المباني تتغير.

وبتزامن مع هذا الهدم، قررت بلدية نابلس أن تهدم ڤيلا مهجورة من تصميم هاني عرفات، وكذلك سينما العاصي التي شيدت في أواسط القرن الماضي. الفرق بينها وبين المبنى الأول أن ملاعب البلدية كانت واحدة من الأمثلة القليلة ذات السمة الاجتماعية للتخطيط الحداثي التي اتخذت شكل تصميم منفتح ومتاح ومنطقي، أكثر من كونه تأثراً نمطياً. رأى شارلي قديس، وهو معماري ينتج اليوم خطوطاً جذابة وبراقة في الطيرة في رام الله، مشروعها امتداداً لمشاريع إعادة

أخبرني رزق خوري، والذي يعرف أيضاً باسم أبو سبيرو، بأن ليس لديه أية رسومات من أيام بدء ممارسته المعمارية. عام ١٩٦٧، داهمت القوات الإسرائيلية مكتبه الواقع فوق بوظة ركب في رام الله. كان خوري واحداً من مؤسسي اتحاد المعماريين الفلسطينيين وموظفاً في بلدية رام الله. تشمل مشاريعه الخاصة منزل حنان عشراوي، والذي صمم بالأصل لوالدها داود ميخائيل. كذلك صمم ڤيلا مصطفى الدجاني في القدس وڤيلا عطالله في الشياح.

أود أن أركز على مشروع منتزه رام الله هنا: كانت مساحة عامة حيوية في حديقة البلدية ولها ملعب ومطعم، كلها تدور حول نافورة من الموزاييك الأزرق. تظلل الحديقة عقدات تشبه المراوح من الخرسانة ترتكز على أعمدة فولاذية مملوءة بالإسمنت ومدهونة بدرجات لامعة من الألوان الأساسية. عندما اكتمل المشروع عام ١٩٦٢، قاد أبو سبيرو سيارة نقل إلى جنين واشترى أربع شجرات أروكاريا زرعها في المنتزه.[٢٣] كان أبو سبيرو مهتماً بأشكال هذه الأشجار الصلبة وأغصانها المتسقة المتناظرة، يقول إنها تشبه شجرة عيد الميلاد

رزق خوري،
أوراق الشجر وأشياء أخرى

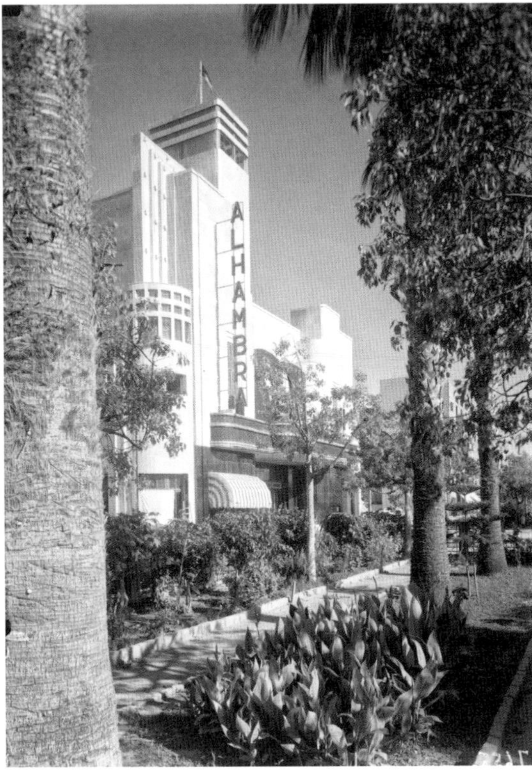
ALHAMBRA

كاتجاه سائد وليس كمشروع».
Bernard Khoury, “Fundamentalists and Other Arab Modernisms,” Divisare website, January 18, 2016, https://divisare.com/projects/307953-bernard-khoury-delfino-sisto-legnani-fundamentalists-and-other-arab-modernisms.
انظر أيضا كتيب المعرض
Architecture from the Arab World: 1914–2014 (A Selection), ed. George Arbid (Manama: Ministry of Culture of Bahrain; Beirut: Arab Center for Architecture, 2014).
وعن تأثير المواد المطبوعة على العمارة في وقتنا، انظر بحث محمد الشاهد عن العمارة وسياسات التحول في مصر ما بين ١٩٣٦ و ١٩٦٧:
Mohamed Elshahed, “Revolutionary Modernism? Architecture and the Politics of Transition in Egypt 1936–1967” (PhD diss., New York University, 2015), ProQuest 3685862.

٧
Mouhanad Hadid, “Architectural Styles Survey in Palestinian Territories” (August 2002), Ministry of Local Government, Palestine National Authority, http://www.molg.pna.ps/ecb/studies/architecture/arch.pdf.

٨ الشكر لخلدون بشارة الذي شاركني هذه القصة وغيرها من القصص عن المبنى المذكور هنا في «طبقة من المظاهر»، وإن كانت القصص أحيانا تقع قليلا خارج الإطار الزمني الذي اخترته.

٩ انظر نص سنان عبدالقادر في دليل العرض الإسرائيلي في بينالي ساو باولو، ٢٠٠٧:
Senan Abdelqader, *Architecture of (in)Dependency*, Israeli Presentation Catalogue, 7th International Architecture Biennial in São Paulo, 2007, http://www.senanarchitects.com/architecture-of-dependency.

يسار:
سينما الحمرا، يافا، شارع جمال باشا، ١٩٣٧

٢ انظر كتاب شارون روتبارد عن الأساطير المرتبطة بعمارة الباوهاوس في تل أبيب، والتي استخدمت في محو مدينة يافا. انظر أيضا الفيلم الوثائقي للمخرج إيال سيفان *Jaffa, the Orange's Clockwork* (٢٠٠٩) وبحث أليساندرو بيتي وساندي هلال وإيال وايزمان (*Decolonizing Architecture*) عن متحف إتزل في تل أبيب والذي بني على أنقاض حي المنشية في مدينة يافا.
Sharon Rotbard, *White City, Black City: Architecture and War in Tel Aviv and Jaffa* (Cambridge, MA: MIT Press, 2015); Eyal Sivan, *Jaffa, the Orange's Clockwork,* 2009, film; Decolonizing Architecture (Alessandro Petti, Sandi Hilal, and Eyal Weizman), *Architecture after Revolution* (Berlin: Sternberg Press, 2013).

٣ انظر مقالة ناصر أبو رحمة:
Nasser Abourahme, "Assembling and Spilling-Over: Towards an 'Ethnography of Cement' in a Palestinian Refugee Camp," *International Journal of Urban and Regional Research* 39, no. 2 (March 2015), 200–17.

٤ مقابلة جورج عربيد مع دين شارب على موقع جدلية، ٢٩ سبتمبر ٢٠١٥:
George Arbid, interviewed by Deen Sharp, "The Arab Center for Architecture (ACA): Interview with George Arbid," *Jadaliyya*, September 29, 2015, http://www.jadaliyya.com/pages/index/22764/the-arab-center-for-architecture-(aca)_interview-wn.

٥ انظر بحث الدكتوراة لشادية يوسف طوقان وكتاب نصير عرفات:
Shadia Yousef Touqan, "Urban Development under Prolonged Military Occupation: The Case of Nablus/Palestine" (PhD diss., Bartlett School of Architecture, University College London, 1995), and Naseer R. Arafat, *Nablus: City of Civilizations* (Nablus: Cultural Heritage Enrichment Center, 2012).

٦ مثلا، واحدة من استنتاجات مشروع برنارد خوري وجورج عربيد في الدورة الرابعة عشر من بينالي البندقية للعمارة أنه «في حين أن بعض المباني التي تعتبر تطبيقات ملهمة للمبادئ الحداثية، يمكن اعتبار بعضها الآخر دليل على النزعة إلى تبني الحداثة

أخيراً خط النهاية. وأخيراً وليس آخراً، الشكر إلى عالم الاجتماعيات سليم تماري، الذي غيرني نهجه المحب والمتواصل تجاه المواد الأرشيفية والتاريخ الاجتماعي، والذي إليه أتوجه بهذا الكتاب.

أخيراً، استمددت طاقتي من صغيرتي ثريا، وهي تزحف على بلاط من طراز آرت ديكو في دار العجلوني التي شيدت عام ١٩٣٣ في رام الله التحتا. منزلي الضخم بشرفاته المدورة المزدانة بحجر بيت لحم الوردي، والمطلة على بساتين الفاكهة (وبدون أي خراطيم ماء تسقي هذه الأرض). ولدعمهم الدائم، أشكر عائلتي: تيرداد وعالية وحنان ورندا وعلاء طوقان وهيا غنمة وعبد عزام وڤيوليت العجلوني، مالكة المنزل التي أضمها إلى عائلتي.

١ نص لمعرض استعادي للفنان في متحف الفن الحديث، نيويورك، ١٩٩٨:
"The Death of Painting," exhibition text for the retrospective "Aleksandr Rodchenko," Museum of Modern Art, New York, 1998, https://www.moma.org/interactives/exhibitions/1998/rodchenko/texts/death_of_painting.html.

انظر أيضا اقتباس للفنان في مقالة ديفيد إليوت في مطبوعة معرض أكسفورد:
Alexander Rodchenko: 1891–1956, exh. cat., ed. David Elliott (Oxford: Museum of Modern Art, 1979).

كانت فعلياً من تصميمه. كذلك أنا ممتنة للمعماريين رزق خوري من رام الله وفؤاد الصايغ من عمّان واللذين ألهماني وحدثاني عن أعمالهما؛ ودائماً وأبداً، للراحل جعفر طوقان الذي أخبرني مرة بأن استراق النظر من فتحات إنارة الحمامات الشعبية في نابلس مرحاً مع أصدقائه كان درسه الأول في فهم العمارة. وهنا، أحب أن أشير إلى تأملات زميلتي داني ليفنتال في الذاتية، وإلى كتاب توم نيكلسون المؤثر العذب «النُصب المقارن (مأمن الله)» (٢٠١٤) عن مقبرة ماميلا في القدس الغربية، وإلى أسلوب ناتاشا صدر حقيقيان في صناعة كتاب الفنان بشكل عام.

كذلك أنا أدين لكل من خالد حوراني ونيكولا بيروجيني وهدى روحانا وإيناس ياسين وكيسي أسبروث-جاكسن وشروق حرب ومهند يعقوبي وإيميليو دابيد وفيرا تماري ويزيد عناني وساندي هلال وشريف واكد وحسن جبارين وفادي أبونعمة وأليساندرو بيتي للعلامات التي تركوها في تفكيري على مدى السنوات الأخيرة، وبالتالي على هذا الكتاب. وشكر كبير لآلاء يونس التي أمسكت يدي لتريني

المتزايد حول الهوية الثقافية الوطنية (والأصلية)، والمواد، وملاءمة الحجر الجيري وكثرته في الجبال الفلسطينية. وأخيراً، احتمالات واستمرارية التفاوض حول القوانين والأنظمة التي تتطلب استعمال الحجر المحلي على واجهات المباني. تجاوز المعماريون بشكل فردي قيوداً مفروضة على الواجهات الخرسانية، في ظل نظام احتلال قيّد بشدة استصدار تصاريح البناء،[٧] من خلال الدعوة إلى حديقة هنا أو مصعد في عمارة تجارية هناك، كما فعل مكتب برغوثي معماريون في مبنى حنانيا وخراز في رام الله.[٨] ومن ضمن الشخصيات التي لم أذكرها ولكنها تستحق بحثاً خاصاً ديران فوسكيريتشيان وأنيس السروجي ومحمد حجازي ومأمون نحاس، ومن زمن أقرب المبدع سنان عبدالقادر الذي تتطور نظرياته وتصاميمه في القدس وإسرائيل باستمرار بالرغم من استراتيجيات جلية للعلن تفرغ المجتمعات الفلسطينية من سكانها.[٩]

أنا ممتنة للمعمارية ريما عرفات ورفقتها التي أرشدتني إلى أعمال والدها الراحل هاني عرفات، والتي أظهرت لي كم من المباني التي اهتممت بها

ولا أرشيفي. منذ البداية، لم أحاول أن أثبت أن هناك «حركة» معمارية حداثية من أي نوع—جزئياً لأنه لو كانت هناك واحدة (في أي مكان، بالمناسبة)، لكانت الحالة الفلسطينية مقزمة ومبتورة: أولاً جراء المشروع الاستيطاني الاستعماري الصهيوني الذي استولى على عِمارة الباوهاوس، ومؤخراً من قبل النيوليبرالية الفلسطينية المتخفية في شكل حركة استقلال. لا بد أنه كان هناك انجذاب قوي تجاه الأشكال الحداثية التي دُرست في القاهرة، وتنوعاتها التي نفّذت في بغداد وبيروت وفيما بعد الخرطوم عبر وسائل اقتصادية وتقنيات محلية.[٤] لكن سمة العصر لا تبدو بأنها كانت مدفوعة بأسباب عقلانية أو اجتماعية أو أيديولوجية، وإنما كانت نماءً عضوياً نابعاً من رموز العمارة المحلية والأنماط التي لحقت الفترة العثمانية والتي بدأت تستخدم أشكالاً مبسّطة (مثلاً، عقدات خرسانية وأنظمة فولاذية تسمح ببناء سقوف مسطحة.)[٥] كذلك يبدو مهماً هنا تأثير الأسلوب العالمي في العمارة كنمط انتشر من خلال مطبوعات صدرت من القاهرة،[٦] إضافة إلى الخطاب

في مدن محتلة ومخنوقة؛ نابلس والقدس وبيت لحم ورام الله وأريحا. هذا التأطير الزمني محصور بين إقامة دولة إسرائيل عام ١٩٤٨، وبين حرب النكسة عام ١٩٦٧، عندما ضمت بقية أراضي فلسطين إلى رقعة دولة إسرائيل. خلال هذه الفترة، هذه الأرض، والتي تعرف باسم الضفة الغربية، وقعت تحت الحكم الأردني. تركت مبانٍ مميزة أنشأت قبل ١٩٤٨ في يافا وحيفا (وحتى اللد والرملة) خارج البحث؛ أشهرها سينما الحمرا في يافا التي صممها الياس المر عام ١٩٣٧، والتي هي مركز العلوم في تل أبيب اليوم. كذلك، لم أورد في البحث مدينة غزة وبيوت الفلسطينيين المطرودين منها والذين يسكنون اليوم في مخيمات الضفة الغربية بحكم من الأونروا. (حتى هذه البيوت، تم مأسستها وتذكرها وحتى الاحتفاء بها في إنشاءات خرسانية داخل مخيمات اللاجئين، حيث لا ينطبق عليها ولا حتى القانون البريطاني الاستعماري الذي يحتم أن تكون ٨٠٪ من الواجهات مبنية من الحجر المحلي.)[٣]

لا يقوم هذا الكتاب على تسلسل زمني ولا نمطي

الشكر موصول لعائلة غوشة وعائلات كنعان والقطب والعالول لكرمهم ومعرفتهم بالتاريخ المعماري لمنازلهم. كذلك أشكر نصير عرفات وشارلي عيسى قديس وأيمن الشكعة ومداخلات جورج عربيد وسحر القواسمي وفداء توما وفيليسيتي سكوت وكاتيا ساندرز وفيليب هوبر. أشكر أيضاً لورا نابير لتصليحها ألوان جزء من هذا المشروع عندما عُرض في معرض مهم في مركز الفن المعاصر في غلاسكو تحت عنوان Shame of Victory (عار النصر)، نسقه ريمكو دي بلاي، والذي كان بدوره فاعلاً أساسياً في بدايات هذا المشروع. شكراً أيضاً لتانيا حبجوقة ويزن الخليلي على اقتراحهما حلولاً نافعة خلال عملية الإنتاج. وأخيراً، أنا ممتنة للدعم الذي قدمته مدرسة رسكن للفن في جامعة أكسفورد، والدعم الذي ناله البحث من كلية سان جون تحديداً، والدعم المالي الذي قدمته مفردات، والذي بدونه لم يكن هذا الكتاب ممكناً.

ما تأتّى من هذه العملية وما سيظهر في هذه المطبوعة هو تجميع لمواد مطبوعة من وحول العمارة، من أواخر الأربعينيات وحتى أوائل السبعينيات، ظهرت

للخطر في الضفة الغربية والقدس الشرقية وغزة؛ بيد أن هذا الأرشيف يتوقف عند عام ١٩٤٨. فهمت من رواق أن الثلاثي الرائع—سحر القواسمي ومهند حديد وإياد عيسى—عمل على مدى عشر سنوات في جمع دليل رواق للأنماط المعمارية الحديثة، وأن المشروع لم يكتمل. لذلك أريد أن أشكر مدير رواق، خلدون بشارة، لتفاؤله الجم وإيمانه بأن كتاب فنان يمكنه أن يكون خطوة تجاه إنجاز سجل للإرث الثقافي الحداثي لفلسطين المحتلة، ولأسلوبه في إعادة استخدام مثل هذه الفضاءات بدلاً من تركها عرضة للهدم. كذلك أحب أن أشكر ريما الكيلاني، لخطتها الساحرة التي مكنتني من استكشاف مواقع في نابلس، وكذلك زهرة زواوي، التي عمقت مفهومي عن «الإرث» عندما مشّتني في شارع فلسطين، وحول سينما العاصي في البلدة القديمة في نابلس، حيث كان دير اللاتين ومجتمعه. عام ١٩٥٢، قام محافظ نابلس، نعيم عبدالهادي، بهدم جميع مباني المنطقة ليفسح المجال لزحف حضري جديد، هو اليوم سلسلة من الواجهات الخلابة التي بنيت في أواسط القرن الماضي.

وبشكل أهم، كانت تولي الأولوية للحركة والانتقال كأداة ضد الحصار والحواجز الإسرائيلية التي تستخدم لحرمان وعزل المجتمعات الفلسطينية عن بعضها.

خلال عملي بالمشروع، تحديداً في ربيع ٢٠١٤، درّست مساقاً في النظرية الوثائقية وركزنا على البدء بدراسة المبنى الذي كنا ندرس فيه: جامعة القدس— معهد الإعلام العصري، بناء حديث رائع كان فيما مضى فندق هيلتون كارلتون رام الله. منذ ذلك الوقت، بدأتْ تتطور قراءات اجتماعية وشخصية وتاريخية متأثرة بتفاعل مع القيّم والكاتب والمعماري يزيد عناني. من خلال تعاونات مختلفة بين الجامعات المختلفة التي درّسنا فيها، أراني كيف تروي المباني قصصها.

تلقيت في عام ٢٠١٥ دعوة من بينالي رواق للنظر في التاريخ المؤسسي للرواق، من خلال مشروع مدته عامان، استخدمت فيه صوري كمادة لكتاب.تعمل مؤسسة رواق مع المجتمع لتوثيق وحفظ وترميم الإرث المعماري الفلسطيني الرازح تحت الاحتلال. احتفي بعملهم عام ٢٠٠٦ من خلال إصدار مطبوعة ضخمة وغنية تسجل المباني التاريخية والمعرضة

«إذا أنت لن تعرفي يافا»، أجابني، «إذا لم تمشي في تل أبيب.» «لكني أمشي في يافا»، أجبت بإصرار. بالمحصلة، ربما كان اهتمامي بتتبع العمارة الحديثة في فلسطين هو محاولة لحل: كيف تتزلزل دلالات أيقونات حداثة ما بعد الحرب—والتي فتح زوجي تيرداد ذوالقدر عينيّ عليها بشكل راديكالي في برلين قبل عشر سنوات—فور أن تقع في سياق فلسطيني؟ ليس كالممثلة التي لم تحمل اسماً في فيلم ألان رينيه حبيبتي هيروشيما (١٩٥٩)، بل لأنني لا يمكنني ببساطة أن «أرى» نفس هذه الخطوط في إسرائيل؛ جزئياً بسبب أن بناء دولة إسرائيل عقّد بشكل عنيف تحويل فلسطين إلى دولة قومية يهودية من خلال استراتيجية مسح معمارية للزمان والمكان، لكي يفسح المجال للدولة الصهيونية.[٢]

بين عامي ٢٠١٣ و٢٠١٥، سجلت بعفوية كل مصادفة مع أشكال تكعيبية ودائرية ومسطحة ومستقيمة وفجة أو غير منمقة في المشهد الحضري الفلسطيني. كانت الصور التي أخذتها في طريقي لا تستحي من ميل خطوطها ومناظيرها. كانت احتفاء بالنظرة الذاتية،

عام ١٩٢١، عرض ألكسندر روجينكو لوحات أحادية اللون، من أحمر وأصفر وأزرق، حتى يشير إلى لا شيء؛ ليقضي على القيمة الشكلية باختصار قصة حياة الشكل إلى تاريخه هو. أدى هذا، بحسب قوله، إلى استنتاج منطقي: «كل مسطح هو محض مسطح وليس هناك من تمثيلات.»[١] كثيراً ما يبدو استخلاص الشكل من التاريخ في فلسطين مهمة مستحيلة، كما حاول روجينكو، لأن للتاريخ نهجه الذي يضرب به جذوره من دون أن يتأثر بمحاولة المرء أن يوقفه لحظياً.

قلت مرة للناشط والخبير اليافاوي سامي شحادة إنني أعرف تل أبيب من صفحات كتب عن عمارتها.

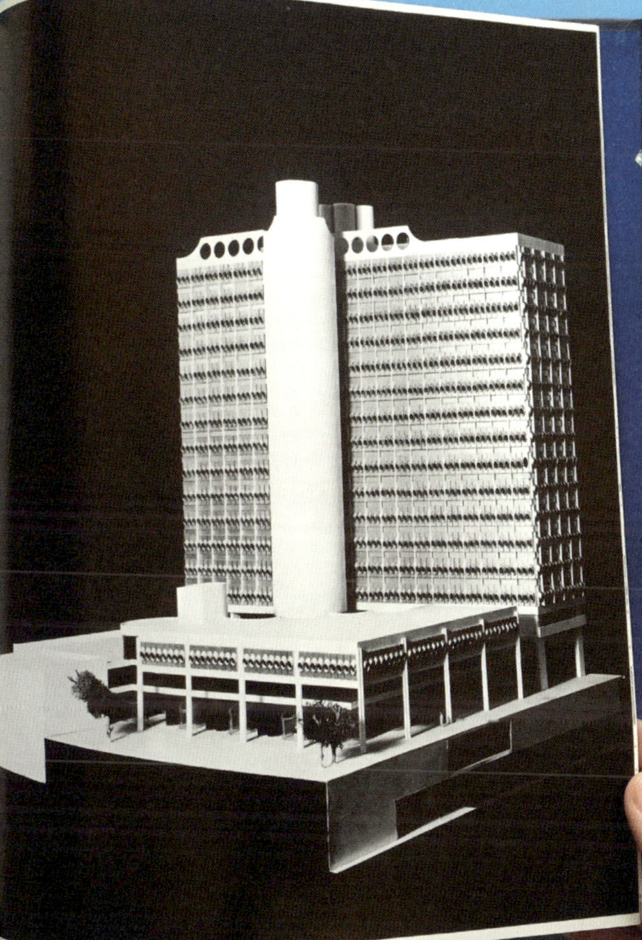

Sundry Modernism
Materials for a Study of Palestinian Modernism

A work by Oraib Toukan

Arabic Translation and Layout
Ala Younis

Copyediting
Zoë Harris, Ayyoub Tams

Publisher
Sternberg Press
Caroline Schneider
Karl-Marx-Allee 78
D-10243 Berlin
www.sternberg-press.com

Printed in Germany
ISBN 978-3-95679-374-5

Image Credits
Cover: Oraib Toukan, Hani Arafat's portfolio.
Pages 18 and 19: "Close Up from the Photographer's Logbook," 1934–39. Eric and Edith Matson Photograph Collection, Prints and Photographs Division, Library of Congress.
Pages 48–113: Oraib Toukan, from the series "Blue Sky Thinking," 2013–15.
Pages 122–57: Courtesy of Reema Arafat.
Pages 167–88: Casey Asprooth-Jackson.
Pages 196–99: Courtesy of Abed Qutob and Khaled Qutob.
Pages 220–21: Courtesy of Charles Kidess.
Pages 224–25: Ramallah City Archives.
Page 232: Eric and Edith Matson Photograph Collection, Prints and Photographs Division, Library of Congress.
Page 245: Oraib Toukan, 2013.

حداثة متنوعة
مواد لدراسة حداثة فلسطينية

عمل لـ عريب طوقان

الترجمة العربية والتصميم
آلاء يونس

مراجعة لغوية
أيوب طمس، زوي هاريس

الناشر
سترنبرغ برس
كارولين شنايدر
جادة كارل ماركس ٧٨
١٠٢٤٣ برلين
ألمانيا
www.sternberg-press.com

طبع في ألمانيا
ISBN 978-3-95679-374-5

حقوق الصور
الغلاف: هاني عرفات. بإذن من ريما عرفات.
الصفحتان ١٨ و ١٩: «صورة مقربة من كتاب المصورين»، ١٩٣٤-١٩٣٩. مجموعة إريك وإديت ماتسون للصور الفوتوغرافية، قسم الطبعات والصور الفوتوغرافية، مكتبة الكونغرس.
الصفحات ٤٨–١١٣: عريب طوقان، من سلسلة «طبقة من المظاهر»، ٢٠١٣–٢٠١٥.
الصفحات ١٢٢–١٥٧: بإذن من ريما عرفات.
الصفحات ١٦٧–١٨٨: كيسي أسبروث-جاكسون.
الصفحتان ١٩٦–١٩٩: بإذن من عبد القطب وخالد القطب.
الصفحتين ٢٢٠–٢٢١: بإذن من شارلي قديس.
الصفحات ٢٢٤–٢٢٥: أرشيف بلدية رام الله.
صفحة ٢٣٢: مجموعة إريك وإديت ماتسون للصور الفوتوغرافية، قسم الطبعات والصور الفوتوغرافية، مكتبة الكونغرس.
صفحة ٢٤٥: عريب طوقان ٢٠١٣.

حداثات

متنوعة

مواد

لدراسة

حداثة

فلسطينية

عريب طوقان

Sternberg Press

Sundry Modernism

Materials for a Study of Palestinian Modernism

Oraib Toukan

Sternberg Press